ROBERT WARD

Robert Ward. Photo by Pach Bros., N.Y.

ROBERT WARD

A Bio-Bibliography

KENNETH KREITNER

BIO-BIBLIOGRAPHIES IN MUSIC, NUMBER 17
Donald L. Hixon, Series Advisor

Greenwood Press
New York • Westport, Connecticut • London

Library of Congress Cataloging-in-Publication Data

Kreitner, Kenneth.
　　Robert Ward, a bio-bibliography / Kenneth Kreitner.
　　　　p.　cm. — (Bio-bibliographies in music, ISSN 0742-6968 ; no.
17)
　　Bibliography: p.
　　Discography: p.
　　Includes index.
　　ISBN 0-313-25701-9 (lib. bdg. : alk. paper)
　　1. Ward, Robert, 1917- —Bibliography.　2. Ward, Robert, 1917—
Discography.　I. Title.　II. Series.
ML134.W28K7　1988
016.78'092'4—dc19　　　　88-24658

British Library Cataloguing in Publication Data is available.

Library of Congress Catalog Card Number: 88-24658
ISBN: 0-313-25701-9
ISSN: 0742-6968

First published in 1988

Greenwood Press, Inc.
88 Post Road West, Westport, Connecticut 06881

Printed in the United States of America

∞

The paper used in this book complies with the
Permanent Paper Standard issued by the National
Information Standards Organization (Z39.48-1984).

10 9 8 7 6 5 4 3 2 1

Contents

Preface

This book is meant to provide a concise but comprehensive
bibliographic guide to the compositions of Robert Ward
through his seventieth birthday in September 1987. As with
the other entries in Greenwood Press's "Bio-Bibliographies in
Music" series, it consists of four main sections.

   (a) a brief <u>biography</u>, prepared with the assistance of
       Dr. Ward;
   (b) a complete list of <u>works</u>, arranged in chronological
       order, with basic bibliographic data, including
       information on the premiere and some selected
       performances. Each work is denoted by the mnemonic
       "W" followed by a numeral indicating its chrono-
       logical position (for example, <u>The Crucible</u> is
       numbered W55), and the performances of that work
       are identified by successive lower-case letters
       (W55a, W55b, W55c, etc.);
   (c) a <u>discography</u> of commercially-produced sound
       recordings of Ward's music, again in chronological
       order, each denoted by the mnemonic "D";
   (d) an annotated <u>bibliography</u> of writings by or about
       Ward and his music, the annotations including,
       whenever practical, excerpts from each item; these
       are in alphabetical order by author, and prefixed
       with the mnemonic "B";

All these sections are cross-referenced with one another, and
they are supplemented by various indexes at the end. With
the exception of the biography, the main sections are
explained in more detail as they come.

The information in the book is in large part based on the
Robert Ward Archive housed in the Music Library of Duke
University in Durham, North Carolina. This collection began
in the winter of 1980-1981, when Dr. Ward, then on the
faculty at Duke, donated his papers to the university. The
original donation was supplemented by a grant from the Mary
Duke Biddle Foundation to aid in the cataloguing of the items

and in the acquisition of additional materials -- chiefly published scores and facsimiles of his music.

The archive now contains almost all of Robert Ward´s surviving work, including withdrawn and unpublished compositions; autograph manuscripts of a great many pieces; a large collection of programs, posters, newspaper clippings, libretti, letters, and other miscellaneous papers surrounding the performances of his music over the years; and an enormous number of the composer´s sketches for music written throughout his career. The collection is invaluable to any scholarly assessment of Ward´s life and works, and it is available to scholars and students. Inquiry should be made to the Robert Ward Archive, Music Library, Duke University, 6695 College Station, Durham, North Carolina 27708.

In the preparation of this volume, which has occupied, off and on, almost four years, I have incurred a number of debts to persons and institutions all across the country. Without any hope of discharging these debts here, I would like at least to acknowledge some of them and express my gratitude.

I am especially grateful to the Mary Duke Biddle Foundation -- both for sponsoring the Ward Archive in the first place and thus making the book possible, and for keeping its author from famine and degradation at two key points along the way. Without the Foundation´s generous and timely support this project would never have been completed.

Frieda Woodruff, now Frieda Gramit, was my collaborator at the initial stages of this work, and though she could not stay on to its completion, a substantial amount of what is here is in fact her work, and the ease and enthusiasm with which I have written the rest owes much to her creativity and patience at the beginning.

Another figure whose influence on this book has been enormous, though perhaps invisible, is J. Samuel Hammond, formerly the music librarian of Duke University. Mr. Hammond was instrumental in the original acquisition and organization of the archive, and his helpfulness and liberality in allowing me access to the materials has gone far beyond the call of duty (and, I fear, sometimes contrary to his natural librarianly impulses). Without his practical help and moral support this might have been an odious task indeed. And fortunately, after his departure from the music library his successors Caroline Usher, Susan Brinn, and John Druesedow were kind enough to continue in his tradition.

Any project of this sort is always plagued with a myriad of niggling little problems -- dates and places to get straight, facts to nail down, foreign languages to be understood, articles to find, and so forth. In my effort to make this work as complete and accurate as possible I have enlisted the help of a legion of friends and connections. Of these I might mention especially Donald Waxman of the Galaxy Music

Corporation; Eleanor Quick and Margaret Knoerr of the East Campus Library, Duke University; Cynthia Turner of Duke's record library; David Mill of the Tufts University Library; Liane Curtis, Jinmi Davidson, Laura Macy, and E.C. Teviotdale of the University of North Carolina at Chapel Hill; and Janet Best, Paul Bryan, David Gramit, Tatsuhiko Itoh, Stephen Jaffee, Stephen Keyl, Lorenzo Muti, Jonathan Stahlke, and R. Larry Todd of Duke University.

I am grateful also to Don Hixon, general editor of this series, for his patience and enthusiasm in helping the project along; and to William Broom, Raymond Knapp, and Michael N. Milone, Jr., for their technical assistance in getting the computer to do what I wanted it to do.

To the people who lived with me and put up with me during the various phases of the task -- my parents, my sister Kitty, and Liane Curtis -- I extend thanks and love and apologies.

But above all I am indebted to Dr. Ward himself -- not only for writing all this music and donating his papers to Duke, but for all the help he has given me as I have struggled to complete it. He has been enormously generous with his time and energy, and his prodigious memory has been invaluable in pinning down elusive facts and names and dates. He assures me that all the hours he has given me over these years were not robbed from his composing. I can only hope he was not just being polite in saying that. I began this project as an admirer and bibliographer; I end it now an unabashed fan.

ROBERT WARD

Biography

Robert Ward was born in Cleveland on September 13, 1917, one
of five children of the owner of a moving and storage
company. As a boy he sang in church choirs and local
operettas, and as a high-school student in the early 1930s he
made his first attempts at composition. (A number of these
early works still survive; see entry W1 in the Works and
Performances section.)

After graduating from John Adams High School in 1935, Ward
spent four years at the Eastman School of Music in Rochester,
New York, studying composition with Bernard Rogers, Howard
Hanson, and Edward Royce. From 1939 to 1942 he attended the
Juilliard School of Music in New York on a fellowship; at
Juilliard he studied composition with Frederick Jacobi,
orchestration with Bernard Wagenaar, and conducting with
Albert Stoessel and Edgar Schenkman. In the summer of 1941
he also studied under Aaron Copland at the Berkshire Music
Center in Massachusetts.

Ward's career as a composer may be broadly divided into three
phases. The first, which extended to the end of World War
II, produced some thirty-seven compositions, of which all but
eleven have been withdrawn. Most of Ward's early works are
on the small scale -- predominantly songs, with a handful of
pieces for piano or chamber ensembles. He did, however,
complete a number of compositions for orchestra, most notably
the First Symphony in 1941, which won the Juilliard Publication Award the following year. Beginning in 1941, Ward
also wrote a number of reviews and other articles for the
magazine Modern Music and served on the faculty of Queens
College.

In February 1942 the composer joined the U.S. Army, where he
was put to work as a musician. His wartime service produced
a number of compositions for the musical organizations he was
conducting. At Fort Riley, Kansas, he wrote a major part of
the score to a musical revue called The Life of Riley, and
after attending the Army Music School at Fort Myer, Virginia,
Ward was assigned to the 7th Infantry and sent to the
Pacific. For the band of the 7th Infantry he wrote a march,

and for its dance band he wrote at least two jazz compositions. Despite their seemingly anomalous place in Ward's
life work, these military compositions were to have an
enduring impact on his musical style: for the next forty
years, in whatever style he chose to write, the influence of
American vernacular music has never been long absent from his
works.

Another unexpected benefit of military service was the
acquaintance of Mary Raymond Benedict, a young Red Cross
recreation worker who (at least according to the composer's
account) was sufficiently impressed with his musical
achievements to take notice of him despite the hordes of
other eligible men in the army. They were married on June
19, 1944, and they have five children.

In between his army duties, which also earned him a Bronze
Star for meritorious service in the Aleutians, Ward managed
to compose two serious orchestral compositions, <u>Adagio and
Allegro</u>, which was first performed in New York in 1944, and
<u>Jubilation -- An Overture</u>, which was written largely on
Okinawa, was finished in 1945, and was premiered at Carnegie
Hall by the National Orchestral Association the following
spring. Both pieces were well received, and the latter
especially has become one of Ward's best-known and most
frequently performed works.

The end of the war marked the end of Ward's musical appren-
ticeship, and the success of <u>Jubilation</u> put him securely in
the ranks of America's most promising young composers. Over
the next fifteen years, the second phase of his career, Ward
worked to fulfill that promise and, not incidentally, to make
a second career as an educator and publisher.

After his discharge from military service, Ward returned to
Juilliard, where he earned his postgraduate certificate in
1946 and taught on the faculty from 1946 to 1956. In
addition, he served as an Associate in Music at Columbia
University from 1946 to 1948, as conductor of the Doctors
Orchestral Society of New York from 1949 to 1955, and as
music director of the Third Street Music School Settlement
from 1952 to 1955. He left Juilliard in 1956 to become
Executive Vice-President and Managing Editor of Galaxy Music
Corporation and Highgate Press in New York, a position that
he maintained until 1967.

Meanwhile, he continued to write music. Three symphonies
appeared during these years -- the Second in 1947, the Third
in 1950, and the Fourth in 1958 -- as well as a number of
other ambitious and significant compositions. The <u>First
Sonata for Violin and Piano</u> was written in 1950, the <u>Sacred
Songs for Pantheists</u> in 1951, <u>Euphony for Orchestra</u> in 1954,
the <u>Prairie Overture</u> in 1957, the cantata <u>Earth Shall Be Fair</u>
in 1960, and the <u>Divertimento</u> the same year.

But the work from this period perhaps most influential on his
later career was his first opera, <u>Pantaloon</u> (later retitled
<u>He Who Gets Slapped</u>), which was premiered in 1956 and revived

three years later, and which marked the beginning of his collaboration with librettist Bernard Stambler, one of Ward's colleagues at Juilliard. It was roundly praised: Winthrop Sargeant of The New Yorker wrote that the opera "was the surprise of the season and, unless I am very much mistaken, marked the entrance into the operatic arena of a composer who is destined to do great things there."[1]

The success of He Who Gets Slapped led Ward and Stambler to look around for another libretto; during rehearsals for the 1959 production, a member of the opera company suggested that they take a look at Arthur Miller's The Crucible, which was having an off-Broadway revival at the time. Off they went, and in the composer's words, "it was one of the most moving evenings in the theater we had ever experienced. The intense drama, sharply-drawn characters, the setting, and the emotional ambiance of the play -- it was everything we were seeking."[2] Mutual acquaintances and the favorable New Yorker reviews secured them an interview with the playwright, and the resulting collaboration led to an opera often regarded as Ward's masterpiece.

Readers of this book will doubtless need no introduction to Ward and Stambler's The Crucible. Since its premiere in 1961, it has been performed dozens, perhaps scores of times, not only in the major American opera houses but in cities as diverse as Iowa City, Wiesbaden, and Seoul. In 1962 it won both the New York Critics Circle citation and the Pulitzer Prize in music, and Winthrop Sargeant's prediction that the opera would "take its place among the classics of the standard repertory"[3] appears to have been amply fulfilled.

The enormous critical and popular acclaim of The Crucible marked another milestone in Ward's career, and the entry into its third phase: from then on, there could be no doubt as to his position among the front rank of American composers. One result of this sudden jump in fame was an outpouring of interest from various ensembles and institutions around the country; of the twenty-seven compositions that have appeared since then, twenty-five bear a dedication or commission.

Many of these, particularly from the 1960s, are what might be called ceremonial works, often written with a particular festive occasion in mind -- for example, Hymn and Celebration (1962), Music for a Celebration (1963), Festive Ode (1966), Fiesta Processional (1966), and Music for a Great Occasion (1970). But the post-Crucible years have seen a good many

---

[1] Winthrop Sargeant, "Oops!" New Yorker 35, no. 12 (May 9, 1959), 161-163, quotation p. 162.

[2] Robert Ward, "A Story of Symbiotic Genius: The Birth of Robert Ward's 'The Crucible'." Listen (program guide to WUNC Radio, Chapel Hill, N.C.), January 1986, 5-9, quotation p. 6.

[3] Winthrop Sargeant, "Big Week," New Yorker 37, no. 38 (November 4, 1961), 179-182, quotation p. 180.

major full-length compositions as well: a cantata, <u>Sweet Freedom's Song</u>, in 1965; the <u>Fifth Symphony</u> in 1976; concerti for piano and tenor saxophone in 1968 and 1984; and no less than four more operas: <u>The Lady from Colorado</u> (1964), <u>Claudia Legare</u> (1977), <u>Abelard and Heloise</u> (1981), and <u>Minutes till Midnight</u> (1982). And just as striking, though on a smaller scale, has been his success with chamber music, particularly in the <u>First String Quartet</u> of 1966 and the <u>Raleigh Divertimento</u> of 1985.

Ward continued as managing editor of Galaxy Music Corporation until 1967, when he became Chancellor of the North Carolina School of the Arts in Winston-Salem. He held this post till 1975, when he stepped down to serve as a member of the composition faculty for five more years. In 1978 he came to Duke University as a visiting professor, and there he remained as Mary Duke Biddle Professor of Music from 1979 to 1987.

It is still too early for a complete critical appraisal of Ward's work as a whole -- partly, of course, because the work is by no means complete, but also because Ward's career has been so long, so prolific, and so varied that any generalization feels premature if not impossible. But a few tentative observations might be made.

Ward has thus far had his greatest success and impact with compositions on the large scale: operas, symphonies, and shorter orchestral works. This is in no way to minimize the quality and quantity of his many songs and keyboard works, most of which are early but some of which are very good indeed, nor especially of his chamber compositions, which are significant but still relatively few. But on the whole Ward seems to have felt more at home in the larger musical forms and with the complexities of the larger ensembles.

His music has always had a distinctly American character, and his life has in many ways exemplified the rise of the American composer in the twentieth century. Ward was among the first generation of composers to receive their entire musical training in the United States, and indeed his most important teachers were native-born Americans as well. From the first poem he set (by Eugene Field) to the latest (by Fred Chappell), he has depended on Americans for most of his texts; and the writers represented in his work make an intriguing anthology of American literature: William Bradford, Edgar Allan Poe, Emily Dickinson, Walt Whitman, T.S. Eliot, and John F. Kennedy, to name only a handful. Four of his six operas are on American subjects, and even his transformation of Ibsen's <u>Hedda Gabler</u> into <u>Claudia Legare</u> involved moving the action of the play from Sweden to South Carolina.

In musical terms as well, listeners will sense Ward's strongly rooted influences in American culture. Like so many

American composers, Ward has remained an eclectic, taking his musical inspiration from a great diversity of sources. This is perhaps most evident in the operas; in The Crucible, to take only the most famous example, the score is indebted here to a Caribbean negro folksong, there to a New England Congregational hymn. And in a great many of his compositions one can hear echoes of a great deal of music outside the western art-music tradition. The Prairie Overture suggests the cowboy song; the saxophone concerto is a study on swing-era jazz (indeed, it even incorporates a tune Ward wrote for his army jazz band almost forty years earlier); moments in the piano concerto evoke the jazz of the 1950s and 1960s most eloquently.

Still, the most conspicuous feature of Ward's oeuvre, and certainly the one aspect that has received the most comment over the course of his career, is its musical traditionalism. Like his teachers Rogers, Hanson, and Copland, Ward has tended to eschew atonality in favor of a style securely rooted in the tonal tradition of nineteenth-century romanticism. His work does, from time to time, pay homage to Schoenberg and his followers -- most notably in the violin sonata, the string quartet, and Sonic Structure -- yet he has never lost sight of his distinct personal style, the eloquent melodies and luxuriant harmonies that have always been his hallmark. Ward's lifelong adherence to the tonal tradition has been praised or condemned by critics according to their preference; but it has been consistently popular with audiences, who continue to find his music not only approachable and agreeable at first hearing, but memorable and satisfying over the long pull.

Again, it is impossible to know exactly what Robert Ward's legacy will be, say, a hundred years hence. Undeniably he has written one very durable opera: a quarter-century after its premiere, The Crucible is being performed more often and more widely than ever, and this in itself is an unusual and impressive distinction among contemporary composers. Many of his other works, some of them dating back thirty and forty years, show signs of similar longevity; they have passed much of the test of time already. And even if he had not written a note, his parallel career in publishing and education -- all the music he has seen through the presses and into the hands of performers, all the musicians and artists and actors he has taught at half a dozen schools around the country -- would surely have its own lasting impact on the future of the arts in America.

The happiest news I can convey in this book is that it promises to be out of date as soon as it appears. In the fall of 1987, when Dr. Ward turned seventy, he retired from Duke University as Professor Emeritus, but he is still active, still healthy, and above all still composing. He and Mrs. Ward continue to live in Durham, North Carolina, and more music is on its way.

Works and Performances

This section provides a separate entry for each composition completed by Robert Ward between 1934 (when he was sixteen) and September 1987 (his seventieth birthday). To this basic objective, however, three provisos must be added. First, twelve student works, dating from 1934 to 1936, have been put together into entry W1 at the composer's suggestion. Second, when part of a larger work has also been published separately -- for example, a single movement of a cantata also printed as a small-scale choral work -- these smaller pieces have not received a separate entry. They can be located by consulting the Alphabetical Index of Titles beginning on page 149.

Finally, and most important, Ward has throughout his career continued to revise earlier works and to reuse old material in his new compositions; on many occasions the lines between retitling, revision, and complete reworking have been difficult to draw. My policy has been to give a piece a separate entry (if only for a cross-reference) if it seems ever to have had an independent existence. In cases of doubt I have been guided by the composer. Again, the Index of Titles should be helpful in finding any piece that seems not to have its own entry.

The entries are arranged in chronological order by date of first completion; for example, the Fourth Symphony, which was completed in 1958 but revised in 1959 and 1977, is placed under 1958. When the same date is given for two compositions, the composer has supplied the chronology.

For each composition, the following information, where applicable and available, has been provided.

> Title. Titles are taken from the printed score or, in the case of unpublished works, from the manuscript. Earlier titles appear in square brackets.

> Date. For most of his works since the late 1930's, Ward wrote the date of completion, usually the month and year, at the end of his manuscript. Some dates have been taken from other written or printed sources, and

in a number of cases I have had to rely on the composer's recollection. Dates that have not been determined precisely are expressed either as seasons ("Spring 1941") or with a question mark ("Feb? 1977").

Agent. Almost all of Ward's compositions since World War II remain available either in printed form or on rental. This line lists the present holder of the rights to each piece; works now withdrawn or in the composer's control are listed as such.

Duration. All durations must of course be regarded as approximate. They are taken from the printed score when possible; otherwise, durations have been timed from recorded performances or calculated from metronome markings.

References. Numbers (e.g. B53) refer to entries in the Bibliography section -- reviews, interviews, articles, and the like -- that refer to the piece itself (as opposed to a specific performance of it).

Genre. A general description of the type of piece or its instrumentation.

Cast. An outline of the cast requirements for dramatic works.

Instrumentation. Instrumentation is given only if it is not obvious from the Genre line (e.g., if a piece is listed as "For string quartet"). Doublings (e.g., a flute part that requires the player to double on piccolo) are not indicated. For an explanation of the abbreviations, see the table on page 73.

Text. Source of text or, in the case of dramatic works, author (and inspiration) of libretto.

Movements. Movements are listed only for works that are clearly divided. The acts and scenes of operas are not included.

Dedication or Commission. These are taken from the printed score or manuscript when possible; some have been provided by the composer, and some initials or first names have been augmented, in square brackets, according to his recollection.

Sketches. Sketches to many compositions are preserved in the Ward archive at Duke University. These have not yet been extensively catalogued or studied; but when available, they are listed here.

Publication. I have tried to list all the forms in which the piece has appeared in print. The matter is an extremely complicated one, however, and some publications may well have eluded my search. Many pieces that have not actually been printed are still available on rental from the agent.

Recordings. Numbers (e.g., D4) refer to entries in the Discography section.

Reworkings. As suggested above, Ward's reuse of his own material has been extensive and complex. A good deal of information on these reworkings has come to light in his writings and in my discussions with him; whatever I have been able to learn and to verify in the scores, I have included in this line. I have not attempted to be comprehensive here, nor to indicate the extent or exact location of each reworking; this material is meant only as a starting-point for future research.

Premiere. By "premiere" I mean to include only the world premiere of the piece, not performances listed as "European premiere," "New York premiere," "Seattle premiere," and so forth. Additional premieres are given only for pieces that exist in two distinct forms (e.g., an orchestral version and a band version). Each entry includes as much information as is available on the date, place, and principal performers; numbers at the end are references to the Bibliography section -- reviews of this performance, articles about it, and the like.

Other selected performances. It is of course impossible to list every performance of every piece Robert Ward has written; many of his compositions are performed several times a year by college bands or church choirs all over the world. In general, a performance is included here if it is referred to by an item in the Bibliography section or if it is represented by a program or another artifact in the archive at Duke University. These later performances are listed in chronological order, and the same information is given as for the premiere. .

W1. [EARLY WORKS]

The following pieces are considered student works, dating
from high school and Eastman. The list includes all extant
compositions that were completed (or nearly completed), but
never formally performed. Dates and chronology are
approximate. All have been withdrawn, and all manuscripts
are at Duke University.

    W1/a. On to Siberia, for piano (1934), incomplete, 34
         mm.
    W1/b. Little Blue Pigeon, for soprano and piano
         (1934), 50 mm. (Text by Eugene Field)
    W1/c. Sarabande, for piano (1934), 40 mm.
    W1/d. Andante, for piano (1934), 25 mm.
    W1/e. Lento, for piano (1934), incomplete, 28 mm.
    W1/f. Moderately (strong rhythm but with great
         freedom), for piano (1934), 46 mm.
    W1/g. Prelude to Al Aaraaf, for soprano and orchestra
         (1935), 136 mm. (Orchestration never finished;
         only vocal score survives; text by Edgar Allan
         Poe.)
    W1/h. Intermezzo, for piano (1935), 56 mm.
    W1/i. Allegro non troppo, for piano (1935),
         incomplete, 36 mm.
    W1/j. Rapidly and delicately (in sporadic flights),
         for piano (1935), 64 mm.
    W1/k. Theme and Variations, for piano (1936), 5
         variations, 83 mm.

W2. THREE SONGS (1934; withdrawn; 6 min.)

    For high voice and piano
    Text by Thomas S. Jones, Jr.
    Movements: 1. I know a quiet vale
             2. Daphne
             3. My soul is like a garden close
    Unpublished; manuscript at Duke University

    Premiere (composer's recollection)

W2a.   1935-6 (Winter): Rochester, New York; Eastman
          School of Music.

W3. FATAL INTERVIEW (Mar 1937; revised Aug 1937; Highgate; 8
    min.)

    Song cycle for soprano and orchestra
    (original) sopr/2.2.2.2/4.2.2.0/eh/bcl/hp/perc/str
    (revision) sopr/3.2.2.2/4.3.3.1/eh/bcl/hp/perc/str
    Text by Edna St. Vincent Millay
    Movements: 1. What thing is this

2. Not in a casket cool with pearls
Dedicated to C[arolyn] R[aney]
Sketches at Duke University
Unpublished; available from Highgate

Premiere (composer's recollection)

W3a.   1937 (April): Rochester, New York; Eastman School
          of Music; Rochester Civic Orchestra; Hazel
          Gravell, soprano; Howard Hanson, conductor.

Other selected performances (composer's recollection)

W3b.   1937 (December): Rochester, New York; broadcast for
          NBC radio; Rochester Civic Orchestra; Arlene
          Hershey, soprano; Guy Harrison, conductor.

W4. EPITHALAMION (May 1937; withdrawn; 3 min.)

For high voice and piano
Text by Percy Blysse Shelley
Unpublished; manuscript at Galaxy Music Corporation

Premiere (composer's recollection)

W4a.   1937 (Summer): Akron, Ohio; private wedding;
          Carolyn Raney, soprano.

W5. Ist STRING QUARTET (1937; withdrawn; 9 min.)

Not to be confused with First String Quartet (1966); see W63.

For string quartet
Movements: 1. Largo -- Allegro
           2. Allegro vivace
           3. Not too slowly
Sketches at Duke University
Unpublished; manuscript at Duke University
Movement 2 reworked into movement 2 of Andante and
     Scherzo (1940); see W14.

Premiere (composer's recollection)

W5a.   1937: Rochester, New York; Eastman School of Music;
          Eastman Quartet.

W6. SLOW MUSIC FOR ORCHESTRA (Nov 1937; withdrawn; 7 min.)

For orchestra
3.2.2.2/4.3.3.1/eh/bcl/cbsn/timp/str
Sketches at Duke University
Unpublished; manuscript at Duke University
Originally planned as movement 3 of a symphony, of

which Ode (1938) was to have been movement 2; see
W7.

Premiere (composer´s recollection)

W6a.   1938 (April): Rochester, New York; Eastman School
           of Music; Rochester Civic Orchestra; Howard
           Hanson, conductor.

W7. ODE (Spring 1938; withdrawn; 6 min.)

For orchestra
3.2.2.2/4.3.3.1/eh/bcl/cbsn/timp/str
Sketches (including unfinished first movement of
    symphony) at Duke University
Unpublished; manuscript at Duke University
Originally planned as movement 2 of a symphony, of
    which Slow Music for Orchestra (1937) was to have
    been movement 3; see W6.

Premiere (composer´s recollection)

W7a.   1939 (April): Rochester, New York; Eastman School
           of Music; Rochester Civic Orchestra; Howard
           Hanson, conductor.

W8. NEW HAMPSHIRE (Sept 1938; withdrawn; 2 min.)

For six women´s voices and string quartet
2soprI/2soprII/2alto/vn/va/2vc
Text by T.S. Eliot
Dedicated to Mrs. Edward MacDowell
Unpublished; manuscript at Duke University

W9. SORROW OF MYDATH (1939; Peer; 4 min.)   See B116.

For high voice and piano
Text by John Masefield
Published: Peer, 1952
Recorded: Desto, c.1963 (D8)

Premiere (composer´s recollection)

W9a.   1939 (Spring): Rochester, New York; Eastman School
           of Music.

Other selected performances

W9b.   1947 (Feb 7): Cambridge, Mass.; Harvard University;
           Nan Merriman, soprano.

W9c.   1947 (Dec 7): Brooklyn, New York; Brooklyn Museum;

          Carolyn Blakeslee, soprano; Margaret Denison, piano.

W9d.   1947 (Dec 22): New York; Carnegie Hall; Kirsten Flagstad, soprano; Edwin McArthur, piano.

W9e.   1951 (Feb 13): Baltimore; Concert Hall, Peabody Institute; Carolyn Bailey, soprano. See B241.

W9f.   1952 (June 11): New Paltz, New York; Lake Mohonk Mountain House; Hazel Gravell, soprano; Joseph Bloch, piano.

W10. AS I WATCHED THE PLOUGHMAN PLOUGHING (Feb 1940; Peer; 3 min.) See B223.

      For high voice and piano
      Text by Walt Whitman
      Sketches at Duke University
      Published: Peer, 1951

      Premiere (composer's recollection)

W10a.   1940 (Spring): New York; Columbia University; Charles Cammock, tenor.

      Other selected performances

W10b.   1947 (Feb 7): Cambridge, Massachusetts; Harvard University; Nan Merriman, soprano.

W10c.   1947 (Dec 7): Brooklyn, New York; Brooklyn Museum; Carolyn Blakeslee, soprano; Margaret Denison, piano.

W10d.   1951 (Feb 13): Baltimore; Concert Hall, Peabody Institute; Carolyn Bailey, soprano.

W10e.   1952 (June 11): New Paltz, New York; Lake Mohonk Mountain House; Hazel Gravell, soprano; Joseph Bloch, piano.

W11. A YANKEE OVERTURE (Apr 1940; withdrawn; 7 min.)

      For orchestra
      2.2.2.2/4.3.2.1/picc/eh/bcl/cbsn/timp/str
      Dedicated to Dick Bales
      Unpublished; manuscript at Duke University

      Premiere

W11a.   1940 (Spring?): New York; Juilliard School of Music; Juilliard Orchestra; Richard Bales, conductor.

W12. <u>HUSH´D BE THE CAMPS TODAY</u> (July 1940; revised 1941;
        Gray; 4 min.)

    For mixed chorus and piano; alternate version (1941)
        for chorus and orchestra
        (orig) chorus satb/pft
        (orch) chorus satb/2.1.1.2/4.3.3.0/eh/bcl/pft/str
        Text by Walt Whitman
        Published: (p-v score) Gray, 1943
        Recorded: Composers Recordings, c.1963 (D7)

    <u>Premiere</u> (composer´s recollection)

W12a.   1942 (Fall): Washington; National Cathedral;
        combined choruses of the Army Music School and
        the National Cathedral; William Strickland,
        conductor. See B42.

    <u>Other selected performances</u>

W12b.   1946 (May 26): Alexandria, Virginia; George
        Washington High School Auditorium; Alexandria
        Choral Society; Louis A. Potter, conductor.

W12c.   1947 (April 29): Rochester, New York; Eastman
        Theatre; Eastman School Junior Symphony
        Orchestra; Eastman School Choir; Paul White or
        Herman Genhart, conductor. See B353.

W12d.   1948 (May 19): Hartford, Connecticut; Bushnell
        Memorial; Connecticut Chorale; Stanley Freeman,
        piano; Herbert A. France, conductor.

W12e.   1951 (May 4): New York; Temple Emanuel; Canadian
        Singers and the Emanuel Choir; Robert Ward,
        conductor.

W12f.   1963 (July 20): Brevard, North Carolina; Brevard
        Music Center; Transylvania Chorus; David
        Buttolph, conductor.

W12g.   1968 (May 21): Winston-Salem, North Carolina; Fine
        Arts Building, Salem College; Singer´s Guild;
        David Partington, conductor.

W13. <u>RAIN HAS FALLEN ALL THE DAY</u> (Aug 1940; Peer; 2 min.)
        See B223.

    For high voice and piano
        Text by James Joyce
        Sketches at Duke University
        Published: Peer, 1951

Selected performances

W13a.   1947 (Feb 7): Cambridge, Mass.; Harvard University;
                Nan Merriman, soprano.

W13b.   1947 (Dec 7): Brooklyn, N.Y.; Brooklyn Museum;
                Carolyn Blakeslee, soprano; Margaret Denison,
                piano.

W13c.   1951 (Feb 13): Baltimore; Concert Hall, Peabody
                Institute; Carolyn Bailey, soprano. See B241.

W13d.   1952 (June 11): New Paltz, N.Y.; Lake Mohonk
                Mountain House; Hazel Gravell, soprano; Joseph
                Bloch, piano.

W13e.   ?? (Apr 6): New York: Carnegie Recital Hall;
                Chloe Owen, soprano; Kenneth Zimmerli, piano.

W14. ANDANTE AND SCHERZO (Fall 1940; withdrawn; 8 min.)

        For string orchestra
        2vnI/2vnII/va/vc/db
        Movements: 1. Andante
                   2. Allegro vivace
        Unpublished; manuscript at Duke University
        Originally written as a string quartet. Movement 2
            reworked from movement 2 of the Ist String Quartet
            (1937); see W5.

W15. ANNA MIRANDA (Nov 1940; revised spring 1987; Highgate; 2
        min.)

        For high voice and piano
        Text by Stephen Vincent Benét
        Unpublished; facsimile of manuscript at Duke
            University

W16. FIRST SYMPHONY (Feb 1941; Highgate; 15 min.) See B29,
        B215.

        For orchestra
        3.2.2.2/4.3.3.1/eh/bcl/cbsn/timp/str
        Movements: 1. Allegro pesante
                   2. Andante
                   3. Allegro
        Sketches at Duke University
        Published: (full score) American Music Center,
            "Juilliard Edition," 1942.
        Recorded: Desto, c.1964 (D10);
                  American Recording Society, c.1964 (D11)
        Originally planned as a string quartet.

Premiere

W16a.   1941 (Dec): New York; Juilliard School of Music;
         Juilliard Graduate School Orchestra; Robert
         Ward, conductor. See B42, B112.

Other selected performances

W16b.   1944 (Spring): Honolulu Symphony Orchestra; Fritz
         Hart, conductor.

W16c.   1948 (Feb 24): Baltimore; Lyric Theater; National
         Symphony Orchestra; Hans Kindler, conductor.
         See B124, B234, B332.

W16d.   1958 (Nov 18, 19): Erie, Pennsylvania; Memorial
         Junior High School Auditorium; Erie Philharmonic
         Orchestra; Robert Ward, conductor. See B1,
         B352.

W17. VANISHED (Spring 1941; Peer; 1 min.) See B223.

         For high voice and piano
         Text by Emily Dickinson
         Dedicated to David Diamond
         Published: Peer, 1951

         Selected performances

W17a.   1947 (Feb 7): Cambridge, Massachussetts; Harvard
         University; Nan Merriman, soprano.

W17b.   1947 (Dec 7): Brooklyn, New York; Brooklyn Museum;
         Carolyn Blakeslee, soprano; Nargaret Denison,
         piano.

W17c.   1951 (Feb 13): Baltimore; Concert Hall, Peabody
         Institute; Carolyn Bailey, soprano. See B241.

W17d.   1952 (June 11): New Paltz, New York; Lake Mohonk
         Mountain House; Hazel Gravell, soprano; Joseph
         Bloch, piano.

W18. FIRST HARVEST (1939-1941)

Title sometimes given to a group of five separate songs
written about the same time:

         Sorrow of Mydath (1939): see W9
         As I Watched the Plougman Ploughing (1940): see W10
         Rain Has Fallen All the Day (1940): see W13
         Anna Miranda (1940): see W15
         Vanished (1941): see W17

W19. TWO PIECES FOR THE PIANO (1941; Highgate for mvt. 1,
      mvt. 2 withdrawn; 3 min.)

      For piano
      Movements: 1. [Allegro] -- sometimes called "Folk
                    Dance," "Song," or "Bagatelle"
                 2. [Andante] -- sometimes called "Angels"
      Unpublished as such; movement 1 published as "Song" in
          Panorama, ed. Alice McElroy Procter (Boston:
          American Music Co., 1953), pp. 26-27. Facsimiles
          of both movements at Duke University.
      Movements 1 and 2 incorporated as movements 1 and 2 of
          Sonatine (c.1948); see W32. Movement 1 reworked
          into Adagio and Allegro (1943); see W27. Movement
          2 reworked into Hymn and Celebration (1962) and
          thence into the First String Quartet (1966); see
          W56, W63.

      Premiere

W19a.   1951 (Feb 13): Baltimore; Concert Hall, Peabody
              Institute; Benjamin Tupas, piano. (under titles
              "Folk Dance" and "Angels.") See B241.

W20. MOVEMENT FOR STRING QUARTET (Summer 1941; withdrawn; 10
      min.)

      For string quartet
      Unpublished; manuscript at Duke University
      Reworked into Adagio and Allegro (1943); see W27.

W21. SLOW (Aug 1941; withdrawn; 4 min.)

      For piano
      Unpublished; manuscript at Duke University
      Reworked into Adagio and Allegro (1943); see W27.

W22. ENERGETICALLY (Fall 1941; withdrawn; 2 min.)

      For woodwind ensemble
      2.2.1.2/1.0.0.0/bcl/pft
      Unpublished; manuscript at Duke University
      Reworked into Jubilation -- An Overture (1945); see
          W28.

W23. THE LIFE OF RILEY (1942; withdrawn)   See B338.

    Musical revue for swing band, men's chorus, and
       soloists
    5sax/3tpt/3trbn/pft/db/dr
    Musical numbers:
        1. By the Numbers (words, Julian Claman; music,
           Robert Ward)
        2. The Life of Riley (words, Julian Claman; music,
           Eddie "Duke" Herzog and Seymour Magenheim)
        3. You Did It (words, Irving Kapner; music, Leo
           Hattler)
        4. Cavalry Song (words, Irving Kapner; music,
           Robert Ward)
        5. Pay Day (words, Julian Claman; music, Robert
           Ward)
        6. Our Corresponding Love (words, Julian Claman;
           music, Eddie "Duke" Herzog)
        7. Final March (words, Julian Claman, Joseph
           Hopkins, Irving Kapner; music, Robert Ward)
    Unpublished; facsimile of vocal score at Duke
       University

W24. THE ROLLING SEVENTH (1943; withdrawn; 4 min.)

    March for band
       [1].0.3.1/4.0.3.1/picc/ecl/2asax/tsax/bsax/3ct/
       euph/perc
    Written for the band of the Seventh Infantry, U.S.
       Army
    Unpublished; manuscript at Duke University

    Premiere (composer's recollection)

W24a.   1943 (Spring): Oahu, Hawaii; Band of the Seventh
       Infantry Division

W25. [UNTITLED: THEME FOR A RADIO SHOW] (1943; withdrawn;
    fragmentary)

    For swing band
    Instrumentation unclear: saxophones, trumpets,
       trombones, rhythm section
    Written for the swing band of the Seventh Infantry
       Division, U.S. Army
    Unpublished; whereabouts of manuscript unknown; 2
       leaves of sketches at Duke University

W26. JUST AS YOU WERE (1943; withdrawn; 7 min.)

    For swing band
    voice/5sax/3tpt/3trbn/pft/db/dr

Text by Robert Ward
Written for "The Statesmen," swing band of the Seventh
    Infantry Division, U.S. Army
Unpublished; manuscript at Duke University
Tune reworked into movement 2 of the Concerto for
    Saxophone (1984); see W81.

W27. ADAGIO AND ALLEGRO (Aug 1944; Peer; 12 minutes)   See
    B309.

    For large orchestra
    2.2.2.2/4.3.3.1/timp/cym/str
    Dedicated to Mrs. Margaret Castle
    Sketches at Duke University
    Published: (full score) Peer, 1953
    Recorded: M-G-M Records, c.1956 (D3)
    Adagio section reworked from Slow (1941) and Two
        Pieces for the Piano (1941); see W21, W19. Allegro
        section reworked from Movement for String Quartet
        (1941); see W20.

    Premiere

W27a.   1944 (spring): New York; Juilliard Graduate School
            Orchestra; Richard Bales, conductor. See B111.

    Other selected performances

W27b.   1946 (May 20): New York; Carnegie Hall; National
            Orchestral Association; Leon Barzin, Conductor.
            See B182.

W27c.   1947 (Dec 23): Nashville, Tennessee; War Memorial
            Auditorium; Nashville Symphony Orchestra;
            William Strickland, conductor.

W27d.   1949 (Nov 27): Washington; Constitution Hall;
            National Symphony Orchestra; Howard Mitchell,
            conductor. See B124.

W27e.   1951 (Feb 14): Baltimore; The Lyric; Baltimore
            Symphony Orchestra; Robert Ward, conductor. See
            B331.

W27f.   1972 (Oct 14): Anderson, Indiana; O.C. Lewis
            Gymnasium, Anderson College; Anderson Symphony;
            John Christopher Cooley, conductor.

W28. JUBILATION -- AN OVERTURE (Summer 1945; Highgate; 10
    min.) See B309.

    For orchestra; alternate version (arr. Robert Leist)
        for concert band
    (orch) 2.2.2.2/4.3.3.1/picc/eh/bcl/cbsn/timp/pft/str

(band) 1.2.4.2/4.2.3.1/picc/ecl/acl/bcl/cbcl/2asax/
   tsax/bsax/4ct/btrb/euph/timp/perc
Sketches (orchestral version) at Duke University
Published: (orch: full score) Associated Music
                Publishers, 1949
                (band: full and cond. scores, parts)
                Highgate, 1958
Recorded: M-G-M Records, c.1956 (D3)
          Composers Recordings, c.1962 (D6)
Reworked from Energetically (1941); see W22.

Premieres

W28a.   1946 (May 20): New York; Carnegie Hall; National
         Orchestral Association; Leon Barzin, conductor.
         (orchestral version) See B182.

W28b.   1958 (July 10): Brooklyn, New York; Prospect Park;
         The Goldman Band; Robert Ward, conductor. (band
         version)

Other selected performances

W28c.   1946 (Nov 21, 22): Los Angeles; Philharmonic
         Auditorium; Los Angeles Philharmonic Orchestra;
         Alfred Wallenstein, conductor.

W28d.   1946 (Nov 24): Beverly Hills, California; Beverly
         Hills High School Auditorium; Los Angeles
         Philharmonic; Alfred Wallenstein, conductor.

W28e.   1946 (Dec 15): Long Beach, California; Long Beach
         Municipal Auditorium Concert Hall; Los Angeles
         Philharmonic Orchestra; Alfred Wallenstein,
         conductor.

W28f.   1947 (Feb 1): Los Angeles; Los Angeles
         Philharmonic; Alfred Wallenstein, conductor.

W28g.   1947 (Apr 29): Nashville, Tennessee; War Memorial
         Auditorium; Nashville Symphony Orchestra;
         William Strickland, conductor.

W28h.   1950 (April 2): Washington; Constitution Hall;
         National Symphony Orchestra; Howard Mitchell,
         conductor.

W28i.   1950 (April 15): New York; Carnegie Hall; New York
         Philharmonic; Igor Buketoff, conductor.

W28j.   1956 (Oct 28): Amherst, New York; Amherst Symphony
         Orchestra; Harold P. Krull, conductor.

W28k.   1957 (February 16): Waco, Texas; Waco Hall, Baylor
         University; Baylor Golden Wave Band; Donald I.
         Moore, conductor.

W28l.   1960 (Sept 23): Oslo, Norway; Filharmonisk Selskaps

Orkester; Fritz Mahler, conductor.

W28m.   1962 (Mar 16): Tampa, Florida; David A. Falk
         Memorial Theater, University of Tampa;
         University of Tampa Symphonic Band; Hunter
         Wiley, conductor.

W28n.   1963 (June 25): New York; Lewisohn Stadium; Stadium
         Symphony; Alfred Wallenstein, conductor.

W28o.   1963 (Aug 2): Brevard, North Carolina; Brevard
         Music Center; Transylvania Symphony Orchestra;
         James Christian Pfohl, conductor.

W28p.   1965 (Jan 23): Mt. Vernon(?), New York; Wood
         Auditorium; Philharmonic Symphony of
         Westchester; John Barnett, conductor.

W28q.   1966 (October 15): Kingsport, Tennessee; Ross N.
         Robinson Junior High School Auditorium;
         Kingsport Symphony Orchestra; Willem Bertsch,
         conductor.

W28r.   1968 (April 16): Nashville, Tennessee; School of
         Music, Peabody College; Peabody Wind Ensemble;
         Henry Romersa, conductor.

W28s.   1968 (June 1): Columbia, South Carolina; University
         of South Carolina; University Symphonic Band;
         James D. Pritchard, conductor.

W28t.   1974 (July 4): New York; Damrosch Park; Goldman
         Band; Richard Franko Goldman, conductor.

W28u.   1975 (Nov 24): Winston-Salem, North Carolina; Wait
         Chapel, Wake Forest University; North Carolina
         School of the Arts Symphony Orchestra; Nicholas
         Harsanyi, conductor.

W28v.   1975 (Nov 30): Raleigh, North Carolina; Jones
         Auditorium, Meredith College; North Carolina
         School of the Arts Symphony Orchestra; Nicholas
         Harsanyi, conductor.

W28w.   1975 (Dec 1): Washington; Concert Hall, Kennedy
         Center; North Carolina School of the Arts
         Symphony Orchestra; Nicholas Harsanyi,
         conductor.

W28x.   1976 (July 17): Interlochen, Michigan; Kresge
         Auditorium, National Music Camp; World Youth
         Symphony Orchestra; George C. Wilson, conductor.

W29. ARIA (1946; withdrawn; 8 min.)

    For chamber orchestra

1.1.1.1/2.1.0.0/str
Unpublished; manuscript at Duke University
Reworked into movement 2 of Symphony No. 2 (1947); see
W31.

Premiere (composer's recollection)

W29a.   1946 (Spring): New York: American Academy of Arts
          and Letters; Leon Barzin, conductor.

W30. LAMENTATION [OF ANCIENT GUILT] (Nov-Dec 1946; Highgate;
     5 min.)

          For piano (as "Of Ancient Guilt," for piano and
          dancer)
          Solo piano version edited by Samuel Sorin
          Dedicated to Judith Martin
          Sketches at Duke University
          Published: ("Lamentation") Merrymount, 1948
                     ("Lamentation and Scherzo," with W41)
     Highgate, 1984; see W83.

          Premieres

W30a.   1947 (May 11): New York; Studio Theatre; Judith
          Martin, dancer; Alvin Bauman, piano. ("Of
          Ancient Guilt")

W30b.   1947 (July 15): New York; Juilliard School of
          Music; Samuel Sorin, piano. ("Lamentation")

          Other selected performances (all "Lamentation")

W30c.   1947 (Oct 9): Washington; National Gallery of Art;
          Samuel Sorin, piano. See B82, B125.

W30d.   1951 (Feb 13): Baltimore; Concert Hall, Peabody
          Institute; Benjamin Tupas, piano.

W30e.   1979 (Feb 24): Winston-Salem, North Carolina;
          Shirley Recital Hall, Salem College; Earl Myers,
          piano.

W30f.   1984 (Feb 28): Buies Creek, North Carolina; Turner
          Auditorium, Campbell University; Cenieth Elmore,
          piano.

W31. SYMPHONY NO. 2 (Oct 1947; Highgate; 23 min.) See B87.

          For orchestra
          2.2.2.2/4.3.3.1/picc/eh/bcl/cbsn/timp/perc/pft-cel/str
          Movements: 1. Fast and energetic
                     2. Slowly

3. Fast
Dedicated to Mary Ward ("to my wife")
Sketches (some under earlier title, <u>Serenade for
Orchestra</u>) at Duke University
Published: (full score) Associated Music Publishers,
1952.
Recorded: Composers Recordings, c.1960 (D4). See B43.
Movement 2 reworked from <u>Aria</u> (1946); see W29.

Premiere

W31a.   1948 (Jan 25): Washington; Constitution Hall;
         National Symphony Orchestra; Hans Kindler,
         conductor. See B78, B81.

Other selected performances

W31b.   1948 (May 16): New York; McMillin Academic Theater,
         Columbia University; CBS Symphony Orchestra;
         Dean Dixon, conductor.

W31c.   1949 (Jan 25): Nashville, Tennessee; War Memorial
         Auditorium; Nashville Symphony Orchestra;
         William Strickland, conductor. See B64, B65,
         B357.

W31d.   1950 (Jan 27, 28, 30): Philadelphia; Academy of
         Music; Philadelphia Orchestra; Eugene Ormandy,
         conductor. See B70, B206, B276.

W31e.   1950 (Jan 31): New York; Carnegie Hall;
         Philadelphia Orchestra; Eugene Ormandy,
         conductor.

W31f.   1950 (Apr 11): Washington: Constitution Hall;
         Philadelphia Orchestra; Eugene Ormandy,
         conductor. See B123.

W31g.   1961 (Apr 21): Newark, Delaware; Mitchell Hall,
         University of Delaware; Delaware Symphonette; J.
         Robert King, conductor.

W31h.   1963 (Feb 17): Sioux City, Iowa; Municipal
         Auditorium; Sioux City Symphony Orchesta; Robert
         Ward, conductor. See B227.

W31i.   1964 (Oct 24): Albuquerque, New Mexico; Fine Arts
         Center, University of New Mexico; UNM Orchestra;
         Robert Ward, conductor.

W31j.   1968 (Jan 17): Oporto, Portugal; Sinfónico do
         Porto; William Strickland, conductor.

W31k.   1973 (Jan 28): Seattle, Washington; University of
         Washington; University Symphony Orchestra;
         Samuel Krachmalnick, conductor.

W31l.   1974 (Nov 14): Durham, North Carolina; Page

                  Auditorium, Duke University; North Carolina
                  School of the Arts Orchestra; Robert Ward,
                  conductor.

W31m.   1974 (Nov 15): Winston-Salem, North Carolina;
                  Crawford Hall, North Carolina School of the
                  Arts; NCSA Orchestra; Robert Ward, conductor.
                  See B221, B286.

W31n.   1976 (Feb 19): Greenville, South Carolina;
                  McAlister Auditorium; Greenville Orchestra;
                  Robert Ward, conductor. See B317.

W32. SONATINE (c.1948; Highgate for mvt. 1, others withdrawn;
          7 min.)

          For piano
          Movements: 1. [Allegro]
                     2. [Andante]
                     3. Fast
          Dedicated to Mark Ward ("for Mark")
          Unpublished as such (but see W19); manuscripts or
              facsimiles of all movements at Duke University
          Movements 1 and 2 incorporated from Two Pieces for the
              Piano (1941); for further information, including
              performances and later reworkings, see W19.
          Movement 3 reworked into movement 1 of Divertimento
              for Orchestra (1960); see W54.

W33. CONCERT MUSIC (Mar 1948; Highgate; 8 min.)

          For orchestra
          2.2.2.2/4.3.3.1/picc/timp/pft/perc/str
          Commissioned by BMI to honor the celebration of the
              25th anniversary of the League of Composers
          Dedicated to Fritz Mahler and the Erie Philharmonic
              Orchestra
          Sketches at Duke University
          Unpublished; available from Highgate

          Premiere

W33a.   1948 (Dec 21): Erie, Pennsylvania; Strong Vincent
                  Auditorium; Erie Philharmonic Orchestra; Fritz
                  Mahler, conductor. See B102.

W34. SERENADE FOR STRINGS (Aug 31, 1948; withdrawn; 15 min.)
          See B179.

          For string orchestra
          str
          Movements: 1. Moderato: Allegro

                    2. Andante
                    3. Vivace
          Dedicated to Hans Kindler and the Kindler Foundation
          Sketches at Duke University
          Unpublished; fascimile of manuscript at Duke
              University
          Movement 1 reworked into Euphony for Orchestra (1954);
              see W43. Movement 2 reworked into Night Music
              (1949); see W37. Movement 3 reworked into movement
              1 of the Fourth Symphony (1958); see W52.

W35. WITH RUE MY HEART IS LADEN (Jan 1949; Highgate; 3 min.)

          For unaccompanied mixed chorus
          Text by A.E. Housman
          chorus satb
          Commissioned by the Juilliard Foundation
          Sketches at Duke University
          Published: Merrymount, 1949.

W36. CONCORD HYMN (Mar 1949; Highgate; 4 min.)

          For mixed voices a capella
          sopr solo/chorus ssattbb
          Text by Ralph Waldo Emerson
          Commissioned by the Juilliard Foundation
          Sketches at Duke University
          Published: Merrymount, 1949; Highgate, 1979

W37. NIGHT MUSIC (Mar 1949; withdrawn; 5 min.)

          For orchestra
          1.1.1.1/2.1.0.0/hp/str
          Sketches at Duke University
          Reworked from movement 2 of Serenade for Strings
              (1948); see W34.

          Premiere

W37a.   1949 (May 29): Washington; East Garden Court,
              National Gallery of Art; National Gallery
              Orchestra; Richard Bales, conductor.

          Other selected performances

W37b.   1949 (Oct 9): Washington; East Garden Court,
              National Gallery of Art; National Gallery
              Orchestra; Richard Bales, conductor. See B126.

W37c.   1951 (Nov 4): Washington; West Garden Court,
              National Gallery of Art; National Gallery
              Orchestra; Richard Bales, conductor.

W38. JONATHON AND THE GINGERY SNARE (Dec 1949; Highgate; 10 min.)

> For orchestra and narrator
> 2.2.2.2/4.3.2.1/timp/perc/str/narr
> Text by Bernard Stambler
> Commissioned by Igor Buketoff
> Sketches at Duke University
> Published: (piano reduction, by Kurt Manschinger)
>   Associated Music Publishers, 1951
> Reworked into Festival Triptych (1986); see W85.

> Premiere

W38a.   1950 (Feb 4): New York; Carnegie Hall; New York
>   Philharmonic; William Bell, narrator; Igor
>   Buketoff, conductor. See B130.

> Other selected performances

W38b.   1951 (Apr 14): Philadelphia; Academy of Music;
>   Norman Rose, narrator; Philadelphia Orchestra;
>   Alexander Hilsberg, conductor.

W38c.   1951 (May 11): New York; East New York Vocational
>   High School; Manhattan Symphonette; Maurice
>   Bonney, conductor.

W38d.   1951 (Dec 8): New York; Assembly Hall, Hunter
>   College; Max Leavitt, narrator; Little Orchestra
>   Society; Thomas Scherman, conductor.

W38e.   1958 (Mar 2): Spring Valley, New York; Spring
>   Valley High School Auditorium; Norman Rose,
>   narrator; Suburban Symphony of Rockland; Edward
>   Simons, conductor.

W38f.   1963 (Apr 4): Daytona Beach, Florida; Peabody
>   Auditorium; Florida Symphony; Henry Mazer,
>   conductor.

W38g.   1975 (Feb 28): Winston-Salem, N.C.; Crawford Hall,
>   North Carolina School of the Arts; John Deyle,
>   narrator; NCSA Orchestra; Robert Ward,
>   conductor.

W39. THIRD SYMPHONY (Feb 1950; revised summer 1950; Highgate;
>   21 min.) See B265, B354.

> Originally for chamber ensemble; revised version for
>   chamber orchestra
> (orig) 2.2.2.2/2.0.0.0/pft/str

(orch) 2.2.2.2/2.1.0.0/pft/str
Movements: 1. Adagio (in original version, Fantasia)
          2. Arioso
          3. Rondo
Commissioned by and dedicated to William Strickland
    and the Friends of Music of Dumbarton Oaks
Sketches at Duke University
Published: (full score, full orch.) Highgate, 1958
Recorded: Remington, c.1955 (D1)   See B53.
          Composers Recordings, c.1966 (D12)

Premieres

W39a.   1950 (March 31): Washington; Dumbarton Oaks; Robert
         Ward, conductor. (original version)

W39b.   1951 (Feb 13): Baltimore; Concert Hall, Peabody
         Institute; Peabody Conservatory Orchestra; Jan
         Tomasow, conductor. (orchestral version)   See
         B241.

Other selected performances

W39c.   1954 (Apr 2, 3): Cincinnati; Music Hall; Cincinnati
         Symphony Orchestra; Thor Johnson, conductor.
         See B13, B66, B154.

W39d.   1954 (Dec 17): Vienna; Grosser Musikvereinssaal;
         Niederösterreichische Tonkünstlerorchester;
         William Strickland, conductor.

W39e.   1958 (Jan 30): Rochester, New York; Rochester
         Philharmonic Orchestra; John Barnett, conductor.
         See B178, B231.

W39f.   1963 (Aug 10): Brevard, North Carolina; Brevard
         Music Center; Brevard Festival Sinfonietta;
         James Yestadt, conductor.

W39g.   1966 (Oct 23): Washington; National Gallery of Art;
         National Gallery Orchestra; Richard Bales,
         conductor.

W39h.   1969 (Jan 29): Charlotte, North Carolina; Ovens
         Auditorium; Charlotte Symphony Orchestra;
         Jacques Brourman, conductor.

W39i.   1969 (Jan 30): Mount Pleasant, North Carolina;
         School Auditorium; Charlotte Symphony Orchestra;
         Jacques Brourman, conductor.

W39j.   1969 (Feb 12): New York; Town Hall; John Barnett,
         conductor.

W39k.   1974 (Dec 14): Charleston, South Carolina;
         Municipal Auditorium; Charleston Symphony
         Orchestra; Lucien De Groote, conductor.

W391.   1974 (Dec 15): Summerville, South Carolina; Alston
          Junior High School Auditorium; Charleston
          Symphony Orchestra; Lucien De Groote, conductor.

W39m.   1978 (Nov 28): Glen Ellyn, Illinois; Performing
          Arts Center, College of DuPage; New
          Philharmonic; Harold Bauer, conductor.

W40. FIRST SONATA FOR VIOLIN AND PIANO (Apr 1950; Peer; 15
     min.) See B45, B91, B320, B328.

          For violin and piano
          Movements: 1. Andante amabile
                     2. Allegro barbaro
          Dedicated to Herbert Sorkin and Brooks Smith
          Sketches at Duke University
          Published: (score and part) Peer, 1952
          Recorded: Musical Heritage Society, 1979 (D17)

          Premiere

W40a.   1950 (June 11): Washington, D.C.; National Gallery
          of Art; Herbert Sorkin, violin; Brooks Smith,
          piano. See B83, B275.

          Other selected performances

W40b.   1950 (Sept 28): New York; Carnegie Hall; Herbert
          Sorkin, violin; Brooks Smith, piano. See B127,
          B171.

W40c.   1951 (Feb 13): Baltimore; Concert Hall, Peabody
          Institute; Gerald Gelbloom, violin; George
          Silfies, piano. See B241.

W40d.   1951 (Apr 11): New York; Town Hall, Juilliard
          School of Music; Nicholas Berezowsky, violin;
          Beveridge Webster, piano.

W40e.   1951 (Dec 9): Princeton, New Jersey; Procter Hall,
          Princeton University; Nicolai Berezowsky,
          violin; Beveridge Webster, piano.

W40f.   1952 (Oct 12): Brooklyn, New York; Brooklyn Museum;
          Herbert Sorkin, violin; Beveridge Webster,
          piano.

W40g.   1958 (Jan 12): New York; Carl Fischer Skyroom;
          Louise Behrend, violin; Katherine Ellis, piano.

W40h.   1959 (May 2): Rochester, New York; Kilbourn Hall,
          Eastman School of Music; John Celentano, violin;
          Orazio Frugoni, piano.

W40i.   1961 (Apr 7): Piermont, New York; Lyric Theatre;
          Herbert Sorkin, violin; Jho Waxman, piano.

W40j.   1965 (May 1): Tuscaloosa, Alabama; Cadek Hall,
          University of Alabama; Julius Hegyi, violin;
          Charlotte Hegyi, piano. See B120.

W40k.   1976 (Apr 13): Rochester, New York; Kilbourn Hall,
          Eastman School of Music; Oliver Steiner, violin;
          Maria Luisa Faini, piano.

W40l.   1980 (May 4): Albany, New York; New York State
          Museum; Capitol Chamber Artists; Mary Lou
          Saetta, violin; John Gaffney, piano. See B322.

W40m.   1984 (Feb 28): Buies Creek, North Carolina; Turner
          Auditorium, Campbell University; James Garner,
          violin; Sherrill Martin, piano.

W41. SCHERZO (Dec 1950; Highgate; 6 min.)

        For piano
        Published (with Lamentation) Highgate, 1984; see W30,
          W83.
        Reworked into movement 3 of Divertimento for Orchestra
          (1960); see W54.

        Premiere

W41a.   1951 (Feb 13): Baltimore; Peabody Conservatory;
          William Chrystal, piano. See B241.

        Other selected performances

W41b.   1979 (Feb 24): Winston-Salem, North Carolina;
          Shirley Recital Hall, Salem College; Earl Myers,
          piano.

W42. SACRED SONGS FOR PANTHEISTS (Jan 1951; Highgate; 15
     min.) See B228.

        For soprano and orchestra; alternate version (ed. Vera
          Brodsky) for soprano and piano
        solo sopr/2.1.3.1/2.2.2.0/hp/str
        Text by Gerard Manley Hopkins, James Stephens, and
          Emily Dickinson
        Movements: 1. Pied Beauty (Hopkins)
                   2. Little Things (Stephens)
                   3. Intoxication (Dickinson)
                   4. Heaven-Haven (Hopkins)
                   5. God's Grandeur (Hopkins)
        Commissioned by the Quincy Society of Fine Arts of
          Quincy, Illinois, and its conductor, George Irwin
        Sketches at Duke University
        Published: (p-v score) Highgate, 1966
        Recorded: Composers Recordings, 1966 (D12)

Premiere

W42a.   1951 (Apr 26): Quincy, Illinois; Moose Hall; Quincy Society of Fine Arts and Quincy Little Symphony; Carolyn Blakeslee, soprano; George Irwin, conductor. See B74.

Other selected performances

W42b.   1951 (Feb 13): Baltimore; Concert Hall, Peabody Institute; Carolyn Bailey, soprano. (preview of mvt.3) See B241.

W42c.   1956 (April 20): West Nyack, New York; Rockland Foundation Studio; Joy Heaton Barker, soprano; Chester Lane, piano. (mvts. 2 and 3)

W42d.   1957 (Oct 3): New York; Carnegie Recital Hall; Rosemarie Radman, soprano; Emanuel Balaban, piano. See B262.

W42e.   1966 (Dec 29): Washington; Grand Ballroom, Mayflower Hotel; Katherine Hansel, soprano; orchestra conducted by Robert Ward.

W42f.   1969 (Feb 2): Chapel Hill, North Carolina; Great Hall, Carolina Union; Jane Sullivan, soprano; Evelyn Coulton, piano.

W42g.   1971 (Sept 24): Winston-Salem, North Carolina; Main Hall, North Carolina School for the Arts; Janice Harsanyi, soprano.

W42h.   1972 (March 26): Philadelphia; Philadelphia Art Alliance; Janice Harsanyi, soprano.

W42i.   1972 (May 7): Utica, New York; Museum auditorium, Munson-Williams-Proctor Institute; Janice Harsanyi, soprano; Margo Garrett, piano.

W42j.   1972 (Oct 23): Misenheimer, North Carolina; Pfeiffer College; Janice Harsanyi, soprano; Margo Garrett, piano.

W42k.   1974 (July 8): Winston-Salem, North Carolina; Crawford Hall, North Carolina School for the Arts; Janice Harsanyi, soprano; NCSA Festival Orchestra; Nicholas Harsanyi, conductor.

W42l.   1984 (Feb 28): Buies Creek, North Carolina; Turner Auditorium, Campbell University; Marian Kennedy, soprano; Cenieth Elmore, piano. ("Pied Beauty" only)

W43. <u>EUPHONY FOR ORCHESTRA</u> (Jan 1954; Highgate; 10 minutes)

> For orchestra
> 2.2.2.2/4.2.3.1/timp/cym/str
> Commissioned by and dedicated to the Louisville
>   Orchestra and its conductor, Robert Whitney
> Sketches at Duke University
> Published: (full score) Highgate, 1957
> Recorded: Louisville Philharmonic Society, c.1955 (D2)
> Reworked from movement 1 of <u>Serenade for Strings</u>
>   (1948); see W34.

> Premiere

W43a.   1954 (Oct 30): Louisville, Kentucky; Louisville
          Orchestra; Robert Whitney, conductor.

> Other selected performances

W43b.   1958 (Mar 30): Pasadena, California; Pasadena Civic
          Auditorium; Pasadena Symphony Orchestra; Richard
          Lert, conductor.

W43c.   1959 (Feb 15): New York; Great Hall, Cooper Union;
          City Symphony Orchestra of New York; Franz Bibo,
          conductor.

W43d.   1961 (April 20): Newark, Delaware; Mitchell Hall,
          University of Delaware; Delaware Symphonette; J.
          Robert King, conductor.

W43e.   1962 (Oct 10): New York; Riviera Terrace; Symphony
          of Musical Arts; Vincent LaSelva, conductor.

W43f.   1962 (Oct 18): Cleveland; Severance Hall; Cleveland
          Orchestra; George Szell, conductor. See B24,
          B146, B149.

W43g.   1964 (July 31): New York; The Mall, Central Park;
          Naumburg Orchestra; Frank Brieff, conductor.

W43h.   1964 (Oct 22): Albuquerque, New Mexico; Civic
          Auditorium; Albuquerque Civic Symphony; Robert
          Ward, conductor. See B204.

W43i.   1967 (Mar 28): Fort Lauderdale, Florida; Fort
          Lauderdale Symphony Orchestra; Emerson Buckley,
          conductor. See B108.

W43j.   1967 (Nov 20): Richmond, Virginia; The Mosque;
          Richmond Symphony; Edgar Schenkman, conductor.

W43k.   1968 (Mar 31): Winston-Salem, North Carolina;
          Auditorium, North Carolina School of the Arts;
          NCSA Student Orchestra; John Iuele, conductor.

W43l.   1971 (Nov 2): Peoria, Illinois; Peoria Symphony
          Orchestra; Harold Bauer, conductor.

W43m.   1972 (Mar 18): Charleston, South Carolina;
          Charleston Symphony Orchestra; Lucien DeGroote,
          conductor. See B214.

W44. ARIOSO AND TARANTELLE (Sept 1954; Highgate; 11.5 min.)
     See B266.

     For cello and piano; alternate version for viola and
        piano
     Movements: 1. Arioso
                2. Tarantelle
     In memory of Hans Kindler for the Kindler Foundation
     Published: (Arioso, cello and piano) Highgate, 1960
                (Arioso, viola and piano) Highgate, 1960
                (Tarantelle, cello and piano) Highgate,
                   1960
                (Tarantelle, viola and piano) Highgate,
                   1960
     Recorded: Musical Heritage Society, 1979 (D17)

     Premiere

W44a.   1955 (Jan 10): Washington; The Textile Museum; Raya
          Garbousova, cello; Theodore Saidenburg, piano.
          See B32.

W45. ADVENTURES IN SHARPS AND FLATS (c.1955; withdrawn)

     Music to accompany a film produced by the Selmer
        Company, manufacturers of band instruments, of
        Elkhart, Indiana. Neither the score nor the film
        has been found.
     Sketches at Duke University
     Reworked into The Lady from Colorado (1964); see W60.

W46. HE WHO GETS SLAPPED [PANTALOON] (Mar 1956; revised 1959;
     Highgate; 2 hrs.) See B345.

     Opera in three acts
     Minimum cast 7 singers, 2 mutes, chorus
     2.2.2.2/4.3.2.0/btrb/timp/perc/hp/str
     Libretto by Bernard Stambler, based on the play He Who
        Gets Slapped by Leonid Andreyev; German version by
        Felix Brentano.
     Sketches (score and libretti) at Duke University
     Published: ("Ballad from Pantaloon," p-v score)
                   Highgate, 1957
                (libretto) Highgate, 1959
                (p-v score) Highgate, 1961
     Recorded: ("Ballad from Pantaloon") New World Records,
        1977 (D16)

Premiere

W46a.   1956 (May 17, 18, 19): New York; Juilliard Concert
         Hall; Columbia University Opera Workshop; Tilly,
         Fred Swanson; Polly, Charles C. Welch; Briquet,
         James Norbert; Mancini, Norman Myrvik and Edward
         Graham; Zinida, Regina Sarfaty; Pantaloon, Paul
         Ukena; Consuelo, Ewan Harbrecht; Bezano, Richard
         Ballard; Baron Regnard, Stephen Harbachick;
         Third clown, Francis Barnard; Fat Lady,
         Charlotte Jones; Barker, James Davis; Rudolph
         Thomas, musical director; Felix Brentano, stage
         director; Frederick Kiesler, scenic director.
         See B88, B103, B140, B200, B219, B311, B312,
         B373.

Other selected performances

W46b.   1959 (April 28): New York; City Center; New York
         City Opera Company; Tilly, Phil Bruns; Polly,
         Paul Dooley; Briquet, Chester Ludgin; Count
         Mancini, Norman Kelley; Zinida, Regina Sarfaty;
         Pantaloon, David Atkinson; Consuelo, Lee Venora;
         Bezano, Frank Porretta; Baron Regnard, Emile
         Renan; The Maestro, Will B. Able; Emerson
         Buckley, conductor; Michael Pollock, stage
         director. See B15, B84, B143, B161, B167, B176,
         B183, B242, B251, B263, B270, B272, B310, B321.

W46c.   1961 (May 31-July 1): Cleveland; Arena Theatre;
         Karamu House; Tilly, J. Jevnikar; Polly, E.
         Love; Count Mancini, Keith Mackey; Briquet,
         Leroy Strawder; Zinida, Delores McCann;
         Pantaloon, Stephen Szaraz; Consuelo, Ruth Kadish
         and Robin Purcell; Bezano, Frank Strain; Baron
         Regnard, Michael Sandrey; Clowns, Patricia
         Curtis, Archie Harris, and Catherine Martin;
         Benno D. Frank, director; Helmuth Wolfes,
         musical director; Maurice Nystrom,
         choreographer. See B23, B148.

W46d.   1973 (April 12, 13, 14): Winston-Salem, North
         Carolina; Reynolds Auditorium; North Carolina
         School of the Arts; Tilly, David Marshall;
         Polly, Lesley Hunt; Mancini, Louis Turner;
         Briquet, Steve Woodbury and Bill Williams;
         Zinida, Donna Stephenson and Janice Harsanyi;
         Pantaloon, Neal Schwantes and William Beck;
         Consuelo, Linda Austin and Renee Evans; Bezano,
         James Hobak; Baron Regnard, Dale Schriemer and
         Charles Eanes; Clown Conductor, John Coggeshall;
         Norman Johnson, musical director; William
         Dreyer, stage director. See B212, B307.

W46e.   1978 (Jan-Feb) New York; Encompass Theatre;
         Pantaloon, Raymond Hickman; Nancy Rhodes,
         artistic director. See B97, B134, B328.

W46f.   1979 (May 11, 12, 18, 19, 25, 26): Bethesda,
         Maryland; Cedar Lane Stage, Cedar Lane Unitarian
         Church; Pantaloon, Ellwood Annaheim; Consuelo,
         Linda Allison; Bezano, David Richie; Count
         Mancini, Vin Kelly; Zinida, Karen Hettinger;
         Briquet, Michael Pinkerton; Baron Regnard,
         William Evans; Clowns, Diane Schultz and Susan
         Juvelier; Terry Glaser, director; Bert Wirth,
         music director. See B5, B105, B144.

W47. FANTASIA FOR BRASS CHOIR AND TIMPANI (Aug 1956;
        Highgate; 12.5 min.)   See B63, B347.

        For orchestral brass and timpani
        0.0.0.0/4.3.2.1/timp
        Commissioned by and dedicated to Juilliard School of
           Music for the celebration of its Fiftieth
           Anniversary
        Sketches at Duke University
        Published: (full score and parts) Highgate, 1957
        Recorded: Musical Heritage Society, c.1973 (D15)

        Premiere (composer's recollection)

W47a.   1956 (Fall): New York; Juilliard School of Music;
         Juilliard Brass Ensemble; Frederik Prausnitz,
         conductor.

        Other selected performances

W47b.   1968 (Jan 17): Winston-Salem, North Carolina;
         Auditorium, North Carolina School of the Arts;
         NCSA Brass Ensemble; Robert Vodnoy, conductor.

W47c.   1968 (Feb 2, 3, 4): Buenos Aires; Conjunto de
         cobres "argentino" de amigos de musica; Alfonso
         Fisica, conductor.

W47d.   1970 (May 18): New York; Mannes College of Music;
         Mannes Wind Ensemble; Simon Karasick, conductor.

W47e.   1970 (Aug 12): Rome; Piazzo del Campidoglio; brass
         choir of the North Carolina School for the Arts
         Orchestra; Dan Ashe, conductor.

W47f.   1974 (April 24): New York; Juilliard School;
         Juilliard Brass Ensemble; Per Brevig, conductor.

W48. WHEN CHRIST RODE INTO JERUSALEM (Nov 1956; Highgate; 3.5
        min.)

        For mixed chorus with soprano solo and organ
        chorus satb/solo sopr/organ

Text paraphrased from the New Testament by Robert Ward
Published: Highgate, 1957

Premiere

W48a.   1957 (Apr 14): Yonkers, New York; St. John´s
          Episcopal Church; St. John´s Episcopal Church
          Choir.

Other selected performances

W48b.   1984 (Feb 28): Buies Creek, North Carolina; Turner
          Auditorium, Campbell University; Campbell
          University Choir; Robert Ward, conductor.

W49. THAT WONDROUS NIGHT OF CHRISTMAS EVE (Apr 1957;
       Highgate; 3 min.)

       For unaccompanied mixed chorus
       chorus satb
       Text by Robert Ward
       Dedicated to Mrs. Wayne G. Benedict
       Published: Highgate, 1957

W50. THREE PIECES FOR NARRATOR AND PIANO BASED ON POEMS FROM
       OLD POSSUM´S BOOK OF PRACTICAL CATS (1957; withdrawn;
       15 min.)

       For piano and narrator
       Text by T.S. Eliot
       Movements: 1. The Song of the Jellicles
                  2. Mr. Mistoffeles
                  3. Of the Awefull Battle of the Pekes and
                     the Pollicles
       Sketches at Duke University
       Unpublished; manuscript at Duke University

       Premiere

W50a.   1957 (Oct 30): New York; Town Hall; Maxim Schur,
          piano; Inga Lind, narrator.

W51. PRAIRIE OVERTURE (Nov 1957; Highgate; 7 min.)

       For concert band; alternate version for orchestra
       (band)2.2.3.2/4.2.3.1/picc/ecl/acl/bcl/2asax/tsax/
          bsax/3ct/timp/2perc
       (orch) 3.2.2.2/4.2.3.1/timp/perc/str
       Orchestral version dedicated to Mr. David Dushkin and
          Kinhaven
       Sketches (band version) at Duke University
       Published: (band: full and cond. scores, parts)

Highgate, 1960
(orch: full score and parts) Highgate, 1964
Recorded: (band) Franco Columbo, 1967 (D13)
(orch) Musical Heritage Society, c1973 (D15)

Premieres

W51a.   1958 (June 26): Brooklyn, New York; Prospect Park;
The Goldman Band; Robert Ward, Conductor. (Band
version)

W51b.   1963 (July): Kinhaven, Vermont; student orchestra;
Adrian Gnam, conductor. (Orchestral version;
composer´s recollection)

Other selected performances

W51c.   1962 (Mar 16): Tampa, Florida; David A. Falk
Memorial Theater, University of Tampa;
University of Tampa Symphonic Band; Hunter
Wiley, conductor.

W51d.   1967 (Nov 14): Davidson, North Carolina; Hodson
Hall, Davidson College; Davidson College Wind
Ensemble; Grier M. Williams, conductor.

W51e.   1968 (Mar 20-26): Spring Tour; Davidson College
Wind Ensemble; Grier M. Williams, conductor.
Mar. 20: Lakeside High School, Atlanta
Mar. 21: Meridian High School, Meridian,
Mississippi
Mar. 22: J.S. Shaw High School, Mobile, Alabama
Mar. 23: Municipal Auditorium, Morgan City,
Louisiana
Mar. 25: Abramson High School, New Orleans
Mar. 25: Destrehan High School, Destrehan,
Louisiana
Mar. 26: Robert E. Lee High School, Montgomery,
Alabama

W51f.   1968 (May 10): Cleveland; Masonic Auditorium;
All-City High School Symphony Orchestra; Robert
H. Rimer, conductor.

W51g.   1970 (April 29): Stony Brook, New York; Gymnasium,
State University of New York at Stony Brook;
University Concert Band; Simon Karasick,
conductor.

W51h.   1971 (Nov 21): Indianapolis, Indiana; Clowes
Memorial Hall, Butler University; Indiana
All-State Orchestra; Igor Buketoff, conductor.

W51i.   1976 (Feb 3, 4): Fort Lauderdale, Florida; Fort
Lauderdale Symphony Orchestra; Emerson Buckley,
conductor.

W51j.   1979 (Apr 29): Lancaster, Pennsylvania; Fulton
          Opera House; Lancaster Symphony Orchestra;
          Robert Ward, conductor. See B203, B313.

W51k.   1979 (Mar 30): Durham, North Carolina; Baldwin
          Auditorium, Duke University; Duke University
          Wind Symphony; Robert Ward, conductor.

W51l.   1984 (Feb 28): Buies Creek, North Carolina; Turner
          Auditorium, Campbell University; Campbell
          University Wind Ensemble; Robert Ward,
          conductor.

W52. FOURTH SYMPHONY (June 1958; revised 1959, 1977;
        Highgate; 24 min.)

          For orchestra
          2.2.2.2/2.2.0.0/timp/hp/str
          Movements: 1. Adagio
                     2. Grave
                     3. Vivo
          Commissioned by and dedicated to Nikolai Sokoloff and
            the Advisory Board of the Musical Arts Society of
            La Jolla
          Sketches at Duke University
          Published: (full score) Highgate, 1977.
          Movement 1 reworked from movement 3 of Serenade for
            Strings (1948); see W34.

          Premiere

W52a.   1958 (Aug 3): La Jolla, California; La Jolla High
          School Auditorium; Musical Arts Society of La
          Jolla; Robert Ward, conductor. See B173.

          Other selected performances

W52b.   1959 (Mar 17): New York; Carnegie Hall; National
          Orchestral Association; John Barnett, conductor.
          See B17, B162, B170, B236, B243, B274.

W52c.   1980 (May 2): Troy, New York; Troy Savings Bank
          Music Hall; Albany Symphony Orchestra; Julius
          Hegyi, conductor. See B107, B244.

W52d.   1980 (May 3): Albany, New York; Albany Palace
          Theatre; Albany Symphony Orchestra; Julius
          Hegyi, conductor. See B107, B244, B323.

W53. EARTH SHALL BE FAIR (May 1, 1960; Highgate; 26 min.)

          Cantata for mixed chorus (or double chorus) and
          children's choir (or soprano solo) with orchestra
          or organ

choir satb/jr. choir/youth choir satb/2.2.2.2/
  4.2.2.0/timp/perc/str
Alternate version for same 3 choirs and organ
Text based on Psalms selected by John Dexter and "Turn
    Back O Man" by Clifford Bax; hymn tune (part 5) by
    Louis Bourgeois, 1551
Movements: 1. Lord, thou hast been our dwelling place
             2. Then the kings of the earth
             3. Thou changest man back to the dust
             4. Earth might be fair
             5. Search me, O God, and know my heart!
Commissioned by and dedicated to the Des Moines
    Council of Churches, Des Moines, Iowa
Sketches at Duke University
Published: (organ-vocal score) Highgate, 1960
          (mvt. 4, o-v score, as "Would Ye Be Glad
            and Wise") Highgate, 1960
Movement 4 reworked into movement 3 of <u>Concertino for
   Strings</u> (1973); see W71.

Premiere

W53a.   1960 (Nov 20): Des Moines, Iowa; KRNT Theatre; Des
          Moines Council of Churches Choirs; Robert Speed,
          organ; Robert Ward, conductor. See B26, B73.

Other selected performances

W53b.   1961 (Nov 26): New York; St. Bartholomew´s Church;
          Jack Ossewaarde, organist and choirmaster.

W53c.   1963 (July 28): Brevard, North Carolina; Brevard
          Music Center; Transylvania Chamber Orchestra;
          Transylvania Chorus and Choral Ensemble; David
          Buttolph, conductor.

W53d.   1964 (May 3): New York; Madison Avenue Presbyterian
          Church; Oratorio and Youth Choirs; Margaret
          McClellan, director of youth choirs; George B.
          Markey, organist and choirmaster; Alfredo
          Antonini, conductor.

W53e.   1965 (Jan 10): New York; CBS Television; Choirs of
          the Madison Avenue Presbyterian Church; George
          Markey, choirmaster; CBS Concert Orchestra;
          Alfredo Antonini, conductor.

W54.   <u>DIVERTIMENTO FOR ORCHESTRA</u> (Sept 1960; Highgate; 14
     min.)

     For orchestra
     3.2.2.2/4.3.3.1/eh/bcl/cbsn/timp/perc/hp/str
     Movements: 1. Fanfare
              2. Intermezzo
              3. Finale
     Commissioned by and dedicated to the Portland Junior

Symphony
Sketches at Duke University
Published: (full score) Highgate, 1966
Recorded: Composers Recordings, c.1964 (D9)
Movement 1 reworked from movement 3 of Sonatine (c.
1948); see W32. Movement 3 reworked from Scherzo
(1950); see W41.

Premiere

W54a.   1961 (Apr 22): Portland, Oregon; Portland Junior
          Symphony; Donald Thulean, conductor.

Other selected performances

W54b.   1967 (May 2): Lawrence, Kansas; University of
          Kansas; Symposium of Contemporary American Music
          Orchestra; George Lawner, conductor. See B39.

W54c.   1970? (May 9): White Plains, New York; White Plains
          High School Auditorium; Westchester Youth
          Symphony; Norman Leyden, conductor.

W54d.   1971 (Mar 6): Corpus Christi, Texas; Del Mar
          Auditorium, Del Mar College; Del Mar Chamber
          Orchestra; Lawrence W. Chidester, director. See
          B314.

W54e.   1979 (April 29): Lancaster, Pennsylvania; Fulton
          Opera House; Lancaster Symphony Orchestra;
          Robert Ward, conductor. (Movement 2 only) See
          B203, B313.

W55. THE CRUCIBLE (Oct 15, 1961; Highgate; 2 hrs.) See B20,
      B87, B316, B325, B342, B364.

      Opera in four acts
      Cast 16 singers, chorus of 6 girls, chorus ad. lib.
      2.2.2.2/4.2.1.0/btrb/timp/perc/hp/str
      Alternate chamber orchestration 2.1.2.1/2.2.0.0/btrb/
          perc/hp/str
      Text by Bernard Stambler, based on the play by Arthur
          Miller; German version by Thomas Martin
      Dedicated to Mary [Ward] and Elizabeth [Stambler]
      Commissioned by the New York City Opera Company and
          its director, Julius Rudel, under a grant from the
          Ford Foundation.
      Sketches (libretto and music) at Duke University
      Published: (libretto) Highgate, 1961
                 (p-v score) Highgate, 1962, 1963
      Recorded: Composers Recordings, c.1962 (D5) See B9,
          B155, B184, B252, B269.

Premiere

W55a.   1961 (Oct 26): New York; City Center; New York City

Opera; Betty Parris, Joyce Ebert; Reverend
Samuel Parris, Norman Kelley; Tituba, Debria
Brown; Abigail Williams, Patricia Brooks; Ann
Putnam, Mary Lesawyer; Thomas Putnam, Paul
Ukena; Rebecca Nurse, Eunice Alberts; Francis
Nurse, Spiro Malas; Giles Corey, Maurice Stern;
John Proctor, Chester Ludgin; Reverend John
Hale, Norman Treigle; Elizabeth Proctor, Frances
Bible; Mary Warren, Joy Clements; Ezekiel
Cheever, Harry Theyard; Judge Danforth, Ken
Neate; Sarah Good, Joan Kelm; Ruth Putnam, Lorna
Ceniceros; Martha Sheldon, Elizabeth Schwering;
Bridget Booth, Beverly Evans; Mercy Lewis, Nancy
Roy; Susanna Walcott, Helen Guile; Emerson
Buckley, conductor; Allen Fletcher, stage
director; Paul Sylbert, scenery; Ruth Morley,
costumes. See B10, B16, B18, B58, B75, B160,
B168, B169, B185, B196, B197, B199, B218, B250,
B253, B260, B264, B268, B273, B278, B351.

Other selected performances

W55b.   1962 (Mar 25, 29): New York; City Center; New York
City Opera; Tituba, Gloria Wynder; Abigail
Williams, Patricia Brooks; Ann Putnam, Naomi
Farr; John Proctor, Chester Ludgin; Reverend
John Hale, John McCurdy; Elizabeth Proctor,
Frances Bible; Mary Warren, Nancy Foster; Judge
Danforth, Jack DeLon; Sarah Good, Hava Pollak;
Emerson Buckley, conductor. See B235.

W55c.   1962 (Apr 12): Georgetown, Delaware; Georgetown
High School Auditorium; New York City Opera
Company; Elizabeth Proctor, Frances Bible; John
Proctor, Chester Ludgin; Mary Warren, Nancy
Foster; Reverend Hale, John Macurdy; Ezekiel
Cheever, Charles Broadhurst; Kurt Saffir,
accompanist and opera coach. (Act II only)

W55d.   1962 (July 31, Aug 1, 3, 4): Iowa City, Iowa;
Macbride Auditorium, State University of Iowa;
Betty Parris, Rachel Stock; Reverend Samuel
Parris, Eric Giere; Tituba, Susan Bales; Abigail
Williams, Murray Englehart; Ann Putnam, Harriet
Aloogian; Thomas Putnam, Larry Schenck; Rebecca
Nurse, Theresa Ruppencamp; Francis Nurse,
Willard Snustad; Giles Corey, William Abbott;
John Proctor, Wayne McIntire; Reverend John
Hale, Allan Kellar; Elizabeth Proctor, Elizabeth
Allen; Mary Warren, Janet Steele; Ezekiel
Cheever, Malcolm Westly; Judge Danforth, Edward
Richmond; Sarah Good, Dierdre Aselford; Ruth
Putnam, Marcia Heasley; Martha Sheldon, Judy
Boyle; Bridget Booth, Kathy Moore; Nancy Roy,
Miriam Stewart; Mercy Lewis, Lois Hutchinson;
Susanna Walcott, Carolyn Eggleston; Herald I.
Stark, musical director; Harrold C. Shiffler,
stage director; John Quinn, Malcolm Westly,

accompanists. See B11, B57, B69, B201, B202, B230, B372.

W55e.   1962 (Nov 16): New York; Carnegie Hall; Eastman Philharmonia; Sylvia C. Friedrich, mezzo-soprano; Kerry McDevitt, baritone; Howard Hanson, conductor. (Act II, scene 2 only)

W55f.   1963 (Feb 14, 15, 16): Cambridge, Massachusetts; Loeb Dramatic Center, New England Conservatory; Rev. Samuel Parris, Richard Firmin; Abigail Williams, Linda Phillips; John Proctor, John Ring; Rev. John Hale, William Day; Elizabeth Proctor, Joy McIntyre; Mary Warren, Mary Lou Sullivan; Ross Reimuller, conductor; Thomas H. Phillips, Jr., stage director. See B31, B220, B348.

W55g.   1963 (Apr 26): Rochester, New York; Eastman School of Music; Eastman Opera Theater.

W55h.   1963 (June 27, 28, 29): Muncie, Indiana; Little Theatre off Riverside, Ball State Teachers College; Little Shoestring Theatre Opera Workshop; Betty Parris, Jeannie Lefeber; Reverend Samuel Parris, Andrew Brown; Tituba, Theresa Greenwood; Abigail Williams, Bonnie Stephan; Ann Putnam, Judy Riggin; Thomas Putnam, Harold Reinoehl; Rebecca Nurse, Dorothy Booth; Francis Nurse, Don Toby; Giles Corey, Paul Cooley; John Proctor, Ralph Kem; Reverend John Hale, Charles Henke; Elizabeth Proctor, Judy Rains; Mary Warren, Marilyn Ast; Ezekiel Cheever, Harold Smith; Judge Danforth, John Meadows; Sarah Good, Cheryl Brown; Ruth Putnam, Carol Jean Mock; Martha Sheldon, Joyce McCray; Bridget Booth, Sally Creagmile; Mercy Lewis, Janet Wright; Susanna Walcott, Jeannie Bristley; John Campbell, musical director; Gilbert Bloom, stage director; Robert Ward, conductor. See B106, B363.

W55i.   1963 (Aug 30): Pittsburgh; Chatham College Chapel; Opera Workshop at Chatham College; Betty Parris, Marietta Dean; Reverend Samuel Parris, Bruce Stigers; Tituba, Judith Weyman; Abigail Williams, Joan Tallman; Ann Putnam, Ruth Ann Gatto; Thomas Putnam, Borge Karlstedt; Rebecca Nurse, Ann Priest; Giles Corey, John Affleck; John Proctor, Paul Straney; Reverend John Hale, Julius Kukurugya; Elizabeth Proctor, Kay Creed; Mary Warren, Rhonda Holm; Ezekiel Cheever, Frank Kerin; Judge Danforth, Thomas Caruso; Sarah Good, Joyce Gift; Ruth Putnam, Florence Mercurio; Martha Sheldon, Judy Barber; Bridget Booth, Jeannette Tagg; Mercy Lewis, Winona Wiczas; Leonard Treash, producer and director; Evan Whallan, conductor; Richard Woitach, piano.

W55j.   1963 (Nov 3): Wiesbaden, West Germany; Hessisches
         Staattheater; Betty Parris, Eva-Maria Kuschel;
         Reverend Samuel Parris, Viktor Remsey; Tituba,
         Maura Moreira; Abigail Williams, Elisabeth
         Szemzö; Ann Putnam, Annemarie Leber; Ruth
         Putnam, Elisabeth Verlooy; Thomas Putnam,
         Gerhard Misske; Rebecca Nurse, Natalie
         Hinsch-Gröndahl; Francis Nurse, Helmut Funken;
         Giles Corey, Reinhold Bartel; John Proctor,
         Heinz Peters; Reverend John Hale, Helmut Ibler;
         Elizabeth Proctor, Dagmar Naaff; Mary Warren,
         Marie-Luise Gilles; Ezekiel Cheever, Walter
         Meiser; Judge Danforth, Hermin Esser; Sarah
         Good, Lotte Munzinger; Susanna Walcott, Irene
         Schreiner; Mercy Lewis, Elisabeth Epperlein;
         Martha Sheldon, Margot Streubel; Bridget Booth,
         Charlotte Krug; Hermann Bauer, conductor.
         (German trans. Thomas Martin: Die Hexenjagd)
         See B113, B261, B279, B300, B315.

W55k.   ? 1963 or 1964: Bern, Switzerland; Stadttheater
         Bern; Reverend Samuel Parris, William
         Whitesides; Abigail Williams, Wendy Fine; John
         Proctor, Gottfried Fehr; Elizabeth Proctor,
         Sabine Zimmer; Judge Danforth, Walter Hesse;
         Walter Oberer, stage director; Max Sturzenegger,
         conductor. (Die Hexenjagd) See B76, B90, B277.

W55l.   1964 (Apr 22, 23, 24, 25): Hartford, Connecticut;
         Millard Auditorium, Hartt College of Music;
         Opera Department, Hartt College of Music; Betty
         Parris, Margaret Kearns; Reverend Samuel Parris,
         Russel Kierig; Tituba, Nicola Campbell and Carol
         Carcieri; Abigail Williams, Elinor Aronson and
         Ida Faiella; Ann Putnam, Natalie Jacobs and
         Maria Talaber; Thomas Putnam, Arthur Thompson
         and Earl Brown; Rebecca Nurse, Virginia Brown;
         Francis Nurse, Donald West and Frederick
         Desjarlais; Giles Corey, David Lester; John
         Proctor, Philip Treggor and Richard Christopher;
         Reverend John Hale, Vashek Pazdera and Thomas
         Love; Elizabeth Proctor, Jeannine Cowles and
         Deborah Keefer; Mary Warren, Joan Glazier and
         Alice Cody; Ezekiel Cheever, Richard GaroFalo;
         Judge Danforth, Joseph Victor Laderoute, Sidney
         Johnson; Sarah Good, Maria Talaber, Sandra
         Mangan; Ruth Putnam, Anne Powell, Shirley McKie;
         Martha Sheldon, Leslie Cole; Bridget Booth,
         Barbara Hughes; Mercy Lewis, Alice Cody, Dawn
         Damon; Susanna Walcott, Jane Wilcox; Moshe
         Paranov, musical director; Elemer Nagy, stage
         director. See B302.

W55m.   1964 (Dec 3, 4, 5, 6): Los Angeles; Schoenberg Hall
         Auditorium, University of California at Los
         Angeles; UCLA Opera Workshop; UCLA Symphony

Orchestra; Reverend Samuel Parris, Joseph
Kolmel; Tituba, Barbara Patton; Giles Corey,
Dale Jergenson; John Proctor, Brett Hamilton;
Reverend John Hale, Alan Gilbert; Judge
Danforth, Richard Lecitt; Jan Popper, conductor;
William Vorenberg, stage director. See B68,
B118.

W55n.   1965 (Feb 23): Oklahoma City, Oklahoma; College
Theatre, Oklahoma College for Women; Elizabeth
Proctor, Virginia Linn; John Proctor, Ralph
Whitworth; Mary Warren, Dianne Hoy; Reverend
John Hale, Rick McMahan; Ezekiel Cheever, Don
Detrick; Virginia Linn, musical director;
Charles Vaughan, stage director; Marta Robottom,
piano. (Act II only)

W55o.   1965 (June 22): San Francisco; War Memorial Opera
House; San Francisco Opera; Betty Parris,
Claudia White; Reverend Samuel Parris, Ken Remo;
Tituba, Barbara Patton; Abigail Williams, Janice
Wheeler; Ann Putnam, Gwen Curatilo; Thomas
Putnam, Brian Turner; Rebecca Nurse, Donna
Petersen; Francis Nurse, David Giosso; Giles
Corey, Robert Glover; John Proctor, Chester
Ludgin; Reverend John Hale, John Macurdy;
Elizabeth Proctor, Frances Bible; Mary Warren,
Linda Newman; Ezekiel Cheever, James Eitze;
Judge Danforth, Robert Nagy; Sarah Good,
Jeannine Liagre; Ruth Putnam, Joyce Hall; Martha
Sheldon, Louise Corsale; Bridget Booth, Sharon
Talbot; Mercy Lewis, Walda Bradley; Susanna
Walcott, Ann Graber; Herbert Grossman,
conductor; Benno D. Frank, producer. See B21,
B44, B110, B226, B330.

W55p.   1966 (Aug 18, 20, 24, 26): Glens Falls, New York;
Queensbury School Auditorium; Lake George Opera
Festival; Betty Parris, Frances Hoggard;
Reverend Samuel Parris, David Bender; Tituba,
Batyah Godfrey; Abigail Williams, Lila Gage; Ann
Putnam, Lois Crane; Thomas Putnam, Richard
Collins; Rebecca Nurse, Joyce Gerber; Francis
Nurse, Edwin Clauss; Giles Corey, Bernard Fitch;
John Proctor, Robert Paul; Reverend John Hale,
J.B. Davis; Elizabeth Proctor, Frances Bible;
Mary Warren, Mildred Fling; Ezekiel Cheever,
Jack Horton; Judge Danforth, David Lloyd; Sarah
Good, Irene Kessler; Ruth Putnam, Joyce Hall;
Martha Sheldon, Linda Phillips; Bridget Booth,
Carol Cramer; Mercy Lewis, Jane Nicholas;
Susanna Walcott, Susanna Martin; Thomas Martin,
conductor; Lee Williams, stage director. See
B49, B101, B217, B249.

W55q.   1967 (Apr 7, 8, 9): San Francisco; Little Theatre,
Simpson College; Betty Parris, Nancy Hamm;
Reverend Samuel Parris, Jean Canny; Tituba,

Patricia Hiss; Abigail Williams, Kathleen
Norsworthy; Ann Putnam, Mary Mark; Thomas
Putnam, Paul Miles; Rebecca Nurse, Sue Parris;
Francis Nurse, George Fowler; Giles Corey,
Michael Pepper; John Proctor, Stanley
Norsworthy; Reverend John Hale, David Walker;
Elizabeth Proctor, Anne Ogan; Mary Warren, Ruth
Compton; Ezekiel Cheever, Fred Holder; Judge
Danforth, Richard McKinney; Sarah Good, Wendy
Borg; Ruth Putnam, Cheryl Meyerhoeffer; Martha
Sheldon, Joanna Pray; Bridget Booth, Chere
Burch; Mercy Lewis, Robyn Swanson; Susanna
Walcott, Laura Halfvarson; Robert L. Larsen,
conductor.

W55r.   1967 (May 3, 4): New York; Hunter College
Playhouse; Hunter College Opera Workshop; Betty
Parris, Sheila Akin; Reverend Samuel Parris,
Bernard Fitch and Evan Thomas; Tituba, Ruth
Elmore and Batyah Godfrey; Abigail Williams,
Lila Gage and Maria diGiglio; Ann Putnam, Gina
Carelli and Catherine Guillery; Thomas Putnam,
Roger Burke and David Gockley; Rebecca Nurse,
Joyce Gerber and Rosalind Levinson; Francis
Nurse, John Anthony; Giles Corey, Gary Glaze and
George Livings; John Proctor, Robert Paul;
Reverend John Hale, Jack Davison and Bruce
Rabbino; Elizabeth Proctor, Anne Woodmansee and
Alice Mary Nelson; Mary Warren, Martha Williford
and Ronana Segal; Ezekiel Cheever, Frank
Redfield; Judge Danforth, Vahan Khanzadian and
Herbert Pordum; Sarah Good, Gail Sheard; Ruth
Putnam, Rae Ramsey; Martha Sheldon, Joan
Johnson; Mercy Lewis, Rosalind Levinson and
Joyce Gerber; Susanna Walcott, Carolyn Stanford;
William Tarrasch, conductor; David Lloyd, stage
director. See B306.

W55s.   1968 (Jan 7): New York; National Arts Club; Thomas
Martin, conductor. (Unidentified excerpt)

W55t.   1968 (Jan 30, Feb 1, 2, 3, 7): Seattle, Washington;
Opera House; Seattle Opera; Betty Parris, Myrna
Kavanaugh; Reverend Samuel Parris, Norman
Paige; Tituba, Archi Ammons; Abigail Williams,
Peggi Bonini; Ann Putnam, Monte Jacobson; Thomas
Putnam, John Duykers; Rebecca Nurse, Elizabeth
Pharris; Francis Nurse, John Mendenhall; Giles
Corey, Theodore Turner; John Proctor, Chester
Ludgin and Robert Paul; Reverend John Hale, Leon
Lishner; Elizabeth Proctor, Frances Bible and
Mary Lueders; Mary Warren, Gloria Cutsforth;
Ezekiel Cheever, Wallace Snellenberg; Judge
Danforth, Dr. Edward Palmason; Sarah Good, Betty
Martin; Ruth Putnam, Patricia Schlosstein;
Martha Sheldon, Caroline Carpp; Bridget Booth,
Susan Krause; Mercy Lewis, Mary Rose Pritchard;
Susanna Walcott, Jan Hiles; Robert Ward and

Henry Holt, conductors; Allen Fletcher, stage
director. See B163, B164, B255, B298, B303,
B304, B305, B350.

W55u.   1968 (Mar 10): New York; New York State Theater,
Lincoln Center; New York City Opera; Betty
Parris, Elizabeth Swain; Reverend Samuel Parris,
Jack DeLon; Tituba, Jacqueline Norwood; Abigail
Williams, Anne Elgar; Ann Putnam, Lois Crane;
Thomas Putnam, Michael Devlin; Rebecca Nurse,
Charlotte Povia; Francis Nurse, Robert Hale;
Giles Corey, Clinton Nichols; John Proctor,
Chester Ludgin; Reverend John Hale, Malcolm
Smith; Elizabeth Proctor, Frances Bible; Mary
Warren, Joan Summers; Ezekiel Cheever, Kellis
Miller; Judge Danforth, John Stamford; Sarah
Good, LaVergne Nonette; Ruth Putnam, Diane
Kehrig; Martha Sheldon, Donna Owen; Bridget
Booth, Marie Young; Mercy Lewis, Lila Herbert;
Susanna Walcott, Arlene Adler; Samuel
Krachmalnick, conductor; Frank Corsaro,
director. See B159, B181, B271, B291.

W55v.   1968 (Mar 29, 30, Apr 3, 5, 6): Sepulveda,
California; Campus Theatre, San Fernando Valley
State College; SFVSC Opera Theatre; Betty
Parris, Candace Nash; Reverend Samuel Parris,
Bart Johnson; Tituba, Isabelle Tercero and Linda
Gomes; Abigail Williams, Shigemi Matsumoto; Ann
Putnam, Judy Gates; Thomas Putnam, John Redmon;
Rebecca Nurse, Trist Hillman and Marilyn Martin;
Francis Nurse, Paul Munsch; Giles Corey,
Clarence Wiggins; John Proctor, Cary Smith and
Chester Ludgin; Reverend John Hale, Larry Cooper
and Gerald Miller; Elizabeth Proctor, Carleene
Mugrdechian; Mary Warren, Anne Turner; Ezekiel
Cheever, William Smith; Judge Danforth, Larry
Jarvis; Sarah Good, Laura Lindenbaum; Ruth
Putnam, Marilyn Anderson; Bridget Booth, Mij
Courtney; Mercy Lewis, Jean Price; Susanna
Walcott, Marjorie Riggs; David W. Scott,
conductor.

W55w.   1968 (Apr 26, 27, 28): Arlington, Virginia; Kenmore
Auditorium; Opera Theatre of Northern Virginia;
Betty Parris, Ellen Buckner; Reverend Samuel
Parris, David Mallette; Tituba, Jacqueline
Norwood; Abigail Williams, Lila Gage; Ann
Putnam, Janice Hassell; Thomas Putnam, Donald
Boothman; Rebecca Nurse, Joan Winden; Francis
Nurse, William Winden; Giles Corey, Clifford
Billions; John Proctor, William Beck; Reverend
John Hale, Richard Best; Elizabeth Proctor,
Elisabeth Farmer; Mary Warren, Joan Patenaude;
Ezekiel Cheever, Robert Williamson; Judge
Danforth, Stafford Wing; Sarah Good, Carol
Cramer; Ruth Putnam, Susan Hoagland; Martha
Sheldon, Ann O´Dell; Bridget Booth, Dorothy

Bickley; Mercy Lewis, Carol Roberts; Susanna
Walcott, Betsy Miller; Richard Weilenmann,
conductor; Adelaide Bishop, stage director. See
B191.

W55x.   1968 (Sept 17, 21, 27, Oct 3, 9): Kansas City,
Missouri; Lyric Theater; Betty Parris, Doris
Holloway; Reverend Samuel Parris, Gene Bullard;
Tituba, Ruby Jones; Abigail Williams, Catherine
Christensen; Ann Putnam, Marlena Kleinman;
Thomas Putnam, Ronald Highley; Rebecca Nurse,
Marlene Wesemann; Francis Nurse, Walter Hook;
Giles Corey, Edgar Nolte; John Proctor, Adair
McGowen; Reverend John Hale, Jim Fleetwood;
Elizabeth Proctor, Janet Meyer; Mary Warren,
Mildred Fling; Ezekiel Cheever, Harry Danner;
Judge Danforth, Richard Knoll; Sarah Good, Carol
Wilcox; Ruth Putnam, Linda Williams; Martha
Sheldon, Shirley Williams; Bridget Booth,
Ardeena Conway; Mercy Lewis, Barbara Adams;
Susanna Walcott, Carole Mehl. See B22, B138,
B139.

W55y.   1969 (May 1, 3): St. Paul, Minnesota; Auditorium
Theater; St. Paul Opera Association; Betty
Parris, Susan Myers; Reverend Samuel Parris,
Karl Brock; Tituba, Hilda Harris; Abigail
Williams, Joan Sena; Ann Putnam, Carol Stuary;
Thomas Putnam, J.B. Davis; Rebecca Nurse,
Carolyne James; Francis Nurse, Benjamin
Matthews; Giles Corey, Herbert Kraus; John
Proctor, Vern Shinall; Reverend John Hale, Paul
Ukena; Elizabeth Proctor, Nancy Williams; Mary
Warren, Linda Phillips; Ezekiel Cheever, Vern
Sutton; Judge Danforth, Vahan Khanzadian; Sarah
Good, Patricia Murray; Ruth Putnam, Harriet
Westrom; Martha Sheldon, Jackie Herberg; Bridget
Booth, Sharon Claveau; Mercy Lewis, Helen
Sandour; Susanna Walcott, Bonita Gilbert; Igor
Buketoff, conductor; John J. Desmond, stage
director. See B132, B136, B142.

W55z.   1970 (Apr 15, 17, 18, 22, 23, 25): Long Beach,
California; Long Beach Community Playhouse;
California State University at Long Beach; Betty
Parris, Patricia Carl; Reverend Samuel Parris,
Robert E. Gray; Tituba, Virginia White; Abigail
Williams, Carol Hatton; Ann Putnam, Patricia
Smith; Thomas Putnam, Bruce Loganbill; Rebecca
Nurse, Jan Bogardus; Francis Nurse, Charles
Yoder; Giles Corey, Michael Cooney; John
Proctor, John Noschese; Reverend John Hale, John
Johnson; Elizabeth Proctor, Janese Hiles; Mary
Warren, Ellen Kronick; Ezekiel Cheever, Dennis
Drew; Judge Danforth, Dean Rhodus; Sarah Good,
Patricia Carl; Ruth Putnam, Barbara Parks;
Martha Sheldon, Andrea Holycross; Bridget Booth,
Susan Tyus; Mercy Lewis, Hillary Maveety;

Susanna Walcott, Elizabeth Davis; Hans Lampl,
conductor; G.L. Shoup, stage director. See B33,
B222.

W55aa.   1970 (Oct 23): Greenville, North Carolina; School
of Music Recital Hall, East Carolina University;
Jane Murray Dillard, mezzo-soprano; Charles
Bath, piano. ("I do not judge you, John" only)

W55bb.   1971 (Jan 21, 22, 23): Cincinnati; Corbett
Auditorium, University of Cincinnati; UC
College-Conservatory of Music; Betty Parris,
Janet Blake; Reverend Samuel Parris, Clyde
Herndon; Tituba, Holly Jeanne Schueneman;
Abigail Williams, Susan Eichelberger; Ann
Putnam, Madeline Carvalho; Thomas Putnam, J.
Chris Moore; Rebecca Nurse, Carolanne Bruetting;
Francis Nurse, David Goodman; Giles Corey, David
Bezona; John Proctor, Gerald Phillips; Reverend
John Hale, Tom Fox; Elizabeth Proctor, Fredda
Rakusin; Mary Warren, Neva Rae Powers; Ezekiel
Cheever, Lawrence Sisk; Judge Danforth, Alan
Boyd; Sarah Good, Deborah Longwith; Ruth Putnam,
Joy Chutz; Martha Sheldon, Ruth Ann Carter;
Bridget Booth, Laura English; Mercy Lewis, Nancy
Duncanson; Susanna Walcott, Brenda Ballard;
Carmon DeLeone, conductor; Jack Rouse, stage
director. See B301.

W55cc.   1971 (Jan 23): Toledo, Ohio; Toledo Masonic
Auditorium; Toledo Opera Association; Betty
Parris, Elin Richardson; Reverend Samuel Parris,
David Bender; Tituba, Jacqueline Norwood;
Abigail Williams, Arlene Randazzo; Ann Putnam,
Ann Cornell; Thomas Putnam, James Billings;
Rebecca Nurse, Charlotte Povia; Francis Nurse,
Josef Gustern; Giles Corey, Herbert Kraus; John
Proctor, Chester Ludgin; Reverend John Hale,
Arnold Voketaitis; Elizabeth Proctor, Louise
Pearl; Mary Warren, Judith Anthony; Ezekiel
Cheever, David Astor; Judge Danforth, John
Stamford; Sarah Good, Sharon Shaw; Ruth Putnam,
Bonita Winsor; Martha Sheldon, Beverly Saba;
Bridget Booth, Sharon Shaw; Mercy Lewis, Alfreda
Rousos; Susanna Walcott, Melinda Marshall; Anton
Coppola, conductor; Lester Freedman, stage
director. See B36, B229.

W55dd.   1971 (Apr 30, May 1): New York; John Brownlee Opera
Theatre, Manhattan School of Music; Betty
Parris, Annie Bornstein; Reverend Samuel Parris,
George Microutsicos; Tituba, Emily Docimo and
Margie Fields; Abigail Williams, Catherine
Malfitano and Molly Melachouris; Ann Putnam,
Phyllis Worthington and Katherine Dome; Thomas
Putnam, James Clamp and Lloyd Thompkins; Rebecca
Nurse, Gloriosa Caballero and Marsha Bagwell;
Francis Nurse, Earl Brown; Giles Corey, Melvin

Brown; John Proctor, Robert Christesen and Ray
Harrell; Reverend John Hale, Ferenz Gaal;
Elizabeth Proctor, Clamma Dale and Sandra
Walker; Mary Warren, Elizabeth Taylor and
Priscilla Baskerville; Ezekiel Cheever, Frank
Careccia; Judge Danforth, James Clark and Juan
Cuevas; Sarah Good, Patricia Ernest and Zoraida
Lopez; Ruth Putnam, Patricia Ernest; Martha
Sheldon, Paula Mondschein; Bridget Booth, Flora
Martin; Mercy Lewis, Zoraida Lopez; Susanna
Walcott, Kathleen Hegierski; Anton Coppola,
conductor; James Lucas, stage director.

W55ee.   1971 (Oct 27, 29): Boston; Lucy Wheelock
Auditorium, Wheelock College; Associate Artists
Opera Company; Betty Parris, Emme Broughton;
Reverend Samuel Parris, Luther Enstad; Tituba,
Ruth Elmore; Abigail Williams, Susan Larson; Ann
Putnam, Elizabeth Phinney; Thomas Putnam, David
Evitts; Rebecca Nurse, Ann Aubin; Francis Nurse,
Ira Bigeleisen; Giles Corey, Rene Rancourt; John
Proctor, Ernest Triplett; Reverend John Hale,
Harris Poor; Elizabeth Proctor, Jan Curtis; Mary
Warren, Diana Roberts; Ezekiel Cheever, Lewis
Perry; Judge Danforth, Alexander Stevenson;
Sarah Good, Carolyn Stouffer; Ruth Putnam,
Christine Noel Whittlesey; Martha Sheldon,
Loretta Giles; Bridget Booth, Gail Campbell;
Mercy Lewis, Irene Elvin; Susanna Walcott, Mary
Ann Sego; Campbell Johnson, conductor; Nicholas
Deutsch, stage director.

W55ff.   1971 (Nov 12, 13, 14): Urbana-Champaign, Illinois;
Festival Theater, University of Illinois;
University of Illinois Opera Group; Betty
Parris, Jo Lynn Fee and June Manners; Reverend
Samuel Parris, Gene Manners; Tituba, Norma
Raybon; Abigail Williams, Phyllis Hurt and
Deborah Truschke; Ann Putnam, Winifred Brown and
Gretchen Fogel; Thomas Putnam, Robert Smith;
Rebecca Nurse, Adrienne Passen and Eileen
Sheridan; Francis Nurse, Carl Glaum and Antonio
Pavao; Giles Corey, Steve Cary; John Proctor,
Ronald Hedlund and Clinton Thatch; Reverend John
Hale, John Stephens and Steve Markuson;
Elizabeth Proctor, Margaret Yauger; the Proctor
children, Ross and Matthew Hurt; Mary Warren,
Susan Chastain and Lee Willard; Ezekiel Cheever,
John Koch and Winslow Hancock; Judge Danforth,
Donald Wiggins; Sarah Good, Donna Nuber and
Carolyn Backus; Ruth Putnam, Kathleen Duck;
Martha Sheldon, June Manners and Jo Lynn Fee;
Bridget Booth, Lucinda Sloan; Mercy Lewis, Mary
Janet Clark; Susanna Walcott, Mary Linduska;
David Lloyd, conductor and director. See B54.

W55gg.   1972 (Feb. 18, 19, 21, 22): Houston, Texas;
Sharpstown Sr. High School (2 performances),

The Kinkaid School (2), San Jacinto Jr. College
(1); Houston Baptist College Opera Company;
Betty Parris, Robbie Atwood; Reverend Samuel
Parris, Edgar Moore; Tituba, Jenny Holtgren;
Abigail Williams, Glorieta Allison; Ann Putnam,
Laura Pease; Thomas Putnam, Bill Colle; Rebecca
Nurse, Bonnie Sue Woolridge; Francis Nurse,
Robert White; Giles Corey, Paul Bedford; John
Proctor, William Guthrie; Reverend John Hale,
Gene Beall; Elizabeth Proctor, Mary Francis
Langford; Mary Warren, Doris Fuqua; Ezekiel
Cheever, Charles Thornburg; Judge Danforth, Tom
Acord; Sarah Good, Jeannette Barker; Robert
Linder, conductor; Lynn Bracewell, stage
director. See B60, B61, B62.

W55hh.   1972 (Dec 6, 8, 10): Cleveland; Kulas Hall,
Cleveland Institute of Music; CIM Opera Theater;
University Circle Orchestra; Betty Parris, Edith
Fearer; Reverend Samuel Parris, Christopher
Smith; Tituba, Jeanne Segal; Abigail Williams,
Margaret Eaves; Ann Putnam, Violet Weber; Thomas
Putnam, Peter Strummer; Rebecca Nurse, Roberta
Merrill; Francis Nurse, John Helyer; Giles
Corey, Thomas Parker; John Proctor, Edward
Payne; Reverend John Hale, Daniel Kold;
Elizabeth Proctor, Margaret Kennedy; Mary
Warren, Jane Buehler; Ezekiel Cheever, Richard
Tuomala; Judge Danforth, Thomas Johns; Sarah
Good, Marcine Behm; Ruth Putnam, Gwendolyn
Dickerson; Anthony Addison, director and
conductor. See B100, B150, B267.

W55ii.   1973 (May 13): Winston-Salem, North Carolina;
Church of Christ; Donna Stephenson,
mezzo-soprano; Lynda Fowler, piano. ("I do not
judge you, John" only)

W55jj.   1973: St. Paul, Minnesota; St. Paul Opera; Betty
Parris, Melanie Sonnenberg; Reverend Samuel
Parris, Clifton Ware; Tituba, Hilda Harris;
Abigail Williams, Noel Rogers; Ann Putnam,
Carolyn Cornell; Thomas Putnam, Harlan Foss;
Rebecca Nurse, Carolyne James; Francis Nurse,
Lewis Woodward; Giles Corey, James Atherton;
John Proctor, Chester Ludgin; Reverend John
Hale, James Christiansen; Elizabeth Proctor,
Nancy Williams; Mary Warren, Sarita Roche;
Ezekiel Cheever, Jonathan Brigg; Judge Danforth,
Karl Brock; Sarah Good, Patricia Parker; Ruth
Putnam, Julianne Cross; Martha Sheldon, Jeanne
Distell; Bridget Booth, Susan Marie Pierson;
Mercy Lewis, Sharon King; Susanna Walcott,
Natalie Chudy; Igor Buketoff, conductor;
Adelaide Bishop, stage director. See B6, B19,
B119, B133, B209.

W55kk.   1973 (Dec 13, 14): Rochester, New York; Eastman
            Theatre, Eastman School of Music; Eastman Opera
            Theatre; Betty Parris, Nadine Pelle and Marjorie
            Merkel; Reverend Samuel Parris, Stanley Cornett
            and Gene Albin; Tituba, Kathryn Medici and
            Nadine Pelle; Abigail Williams, Suzanne Blum and
            Vicki Snyder; Ann Putnam, Susan Pierson and
            Patricia Richards; Thomas Putnam, Robert
            Freedman and John Oliver; Rebecca Nurse, Jana
            Elam and Kathryn Medici; Francis Nurse, Peter
            Jonas and Dennis Maxfield; Giles Corey, John
            Denison and Michael Crouse; John Proctor, Robert
            Downes and Richard Reif; Reverend John Hale,
            James Courtney and Jay Stearns; Elizabeth
            Proctor, Laura Angus and Sharon Schultz; Mary
            Warren, Candice Baranowski and Elizabeth
            Richards; Ezekiel Cheever, James Pugh and Robert
            Rowland; Judge Danforth, Michael Crouse and
            James Pugh; Sarah Good, Janet Graves-Wright and
            Joanne Dawson; Ruth Putnam, Nancy Hablett and
            Debra Vanderlinde; Martha Sheldon, Constance
            Rylee and Ruth Weniger; Bridget Booth, Deborah
            Bendixen and Janis Hawkins; Mercy Lewis, Sharon
            Schultz and Laura Angus; Susanna Walcott,
            Melissa Miles and Jana Elam; Gustav Meier,
            conductor; Leonard Treash, stage director. See
            B333.

W55ll.   1974 (March 11, 16): Miami, Florida; Dade County
            Auditorium; Greater Miami International Opera;
            Betty Parris, Jane Coleman; Reverend Samuel
            Parris, Norman Paige; Tituba, Hilda Harris;
            Abigail Williams, Louise Russell; Ann Putnam,
            Juliette Wesley; Thomas Putnam, William Beck;
            Rebecca Nurse, Mikki Shiff; Francis Nurse, Hugh
            Thompson; Giles Corey, James McCray; John
            Proctor, Chester Ludgin; Reverend John Hale,
            Arnold Voketaitis; Elizabeth Proctor, Beverly
            Wolff; Mary Warren, Rebecca Roberts; Ezekiel
            Cheever, Jack Horton; Judge Danforth, John
            Stamford; Sarah Good, Sheryl Overholt; Ruth
            Putnam, Theresa Rivera; Martha Sheldon, Linda Jo
            Booker; Bridget Booth, Toni Evers; Mercy Lewis,
            Patricia McCaffrey; Susanna Walcott, Carol
            Andrews; Emerson Buckley, conductor; James
            Lucas, stage director. See B30, B109, B232,
            B256, B258.

W55mm.   1974 (June 28): Des Moines, Iowa; Des Moines
            Metropolitan Opera; Abigail Williams, Mary
            Elizabeth Poore; Thomas Putnam, Robert Benton;
            John Proctor, Robert Paul; Elizabeth Proctor,
            Victoria Villamil; Robert L. Larsen, conductor.
            See B98.

W55nn.   ? c.1975: Boulder, Colorado; University Theatre,
            University of Colorado; University Theatre
            Opera; Reverend Samuel Parris, John Day; Tituba,

Elsie Moore; Abigail Williams, Cynthia Teague;
Thomas Putnam, Bruce Gibson; John Proctor,
Dennis Jackson; Elizabeth Proctor, Kay Fowler;
Mary Warren, Theresa Radomsky; Giora Bernstein,
conductor; Kuniaki Hata, stage director. See
B117.

W55oo.   1975 (May 9, 10, 16): San Diego, California;
Dramatic Arts Theatre, San Diego State
University; Music Department, SDSU; Cleve K.
Genzlinger, conductor; Lyman C. Hurd, stage
director.

W55pp.   1975 (Aug 28, 30): Vienna, Virginia; Wolf Trap
Farm; Wolf Trap Company; Betty Parris, Deborah
Martin; Reverend Samuel Parris, Dean Shoff;
Tituba, Joy Blackett; Abigail Williams, Susan
Smith; Ann Putnam, Patricia Lynne Stone; Thomas
Putnam, Robert Orth; Rebecca Nurse, Judith
Christin; Francis Nurse, J. Scott Brumit; Giles
Corey, Robert Schimek; John Proctor, Richard
Cross; Reverend John Hale, James Courtney;
Elizabeth Proctor, Sheila Nadler; Mary Warren,
Judith James; Ezekiel Cheever, Michael Philip
Davis; Judge Danforth, Alan Crofoot; Sarah Good,
Christine Whittlesey; Ruth Putnam, Nan Polanski;
Martha Sheldon, Susan Chastain; Bridget Booth,
Karen Yarmat; Mercy Lewis, Janice Meyerson;
Susanna Walcott, Margaret Johnson; Christopher
Keene, conductor; Richard Pearlman, stage
director. See B190, B192.

W55qq.   1976 (Jan 29, 31): Pittsburgh; Heinz Hall for the
Performing Arts; Pittsburgh Opera; Betty Parris,
Corinne Salon; Reverend Samuel Parris, Norman
Paige; Tituba, Hilda Harris; Abigail Williams,
Karan Armstrong; Ann Putnam, Chloe Owen; Thomas
Putnam, Alfred Anderson; Rebecca Nurse, Julia
May; Francis Nurse, Paul Schmidt; Giles Corey,
Arthur Graham; John Proctor, Julian Patrick;
Reverend John Hale, Will Roy; Elizabeth Proctor,
Mildred Miller; Mary Warren, Gwenlynn Little;
Ezekiel Cheever, Frank Kerin; Judge Danforth,
Alan Crofoot; Sarah Good, Betty Packer; Ruth
Putnam, Judi Braun; Martha Sheldon, Jessica
Flynn; Bridget Booth, Marcy Sloan; Mercy Lewis,
Jimmie Lu Null; Susanna Walcott, Mimi Lerner;
Robert Ward, conductor; Barbara Karp, stage
director. See B7, B8, B55, B56.

W55rr.   1976 (Feb 7, 8): Jacksonville, Florida; Civic
Auditorium Theatre; Opera Repertory Group. See
B129.

W55ss.   1976 (Mar 18, 20): Milwaukee; Florentine Opera;
Reverend Samuel Parris, Dan Nelson; Tituba,
Hilda Harris; Abigail Williams, Louise Russell;
Ann Putnam, AnnDre House; Rebecca Nurse, Judith

Erikson; John Proctor, Chester Ludgin; Reverend
John Hale, Arnold Voketatis; Elizabeth Proctor,
Beverly Wolff; Judge Danforth, John Stamford;
John Covelli, conductor; James Lucas, stage
director. See B95, B151.

W55tt.   1976 (July 30, Aug 2): Chautauqua, New York; Norton
           Memorial Hall; Chautauqua Opera Association;
           Betty Parris, Christine Isley; Reverend Samuel
           Parris, Richard Brunner; Tituba, Carolyn
           Stanford; Abigail Williams, Marianna Christos;
           Ann Putnam, Dana McKay; Thomas Putnam, Paul
           Yoder; Rebecca Nurse, Jane Shaulis; Francis
           Nurse, Jason Stearns; Giles Corey, Michael
           Crouse; John Proctor, Raeder Anderson; Reverend
           John Hale, Edward White; Elizabeth Proctor, Mary
           Lee Farris; Mary Warren, Janet Pranschke;
           Ezekiel Cheever, Thomas Poole; Judge Danforth,
           Harold McAulliffe; Sarah Good, Judith Balo; Ruth
           Putnam, Christine Flasch; Martha Sheldon,
           Marianne Wells; Bridget Booth, Judith Balo;
           Mercy Lewis, Linda Kowalski; Susanna Walcott,
           Maxine Davis; Wolfgang Schanzer, conductor;
           Whitfield Lloyd, stage director. See B59.

W55uu.   1976 (Nov 18, 19, 20, 21): Ann Arbor, Michigan;
           Lydia Mendelssohn Theatre, University of
           Michigan; Betty Parris, Margaret Schnell and
           Pamela Green; Reverend Samuel Parris, Randy
           Lambert and Joel Dulyea; Tituba, Blanche Foreman
           and Dorian Morris; Abigail Williams, Susan
           Kivela and Kay Murray; Ann Putnam, Lauren Wagner
           and Jacqueline Green; Thomas Putnam, Stephen
           Poulos and Martin Britsch; Rebecca Nurse, Carol
           Madalin and Kathleen Segar; Francis Nurse,
           Charles Brown and Lawrence Albert; Giles Corey,
           John Littlefield and Robin Morisi; Reverend John
           Hale, Carlos Chausson and Stephen Bryant;
           Elizabeth Proctor, Lorraine Manz and Laura
           Holland; Mary Warren, Lauran Fulton and
           Bernadine Oakley; Ezekiel Cheever, Joel Dulyea
           and Gene Sager; Judge Danforth, James Russey and
           Randy Lambert; Sarah Good, Gloria Hill and Susan
           Anthony; Ruth Putnam, Bettina Isaacson; Martha
           Sheldon, Eileen Moreman; Bridget Booth,
           Gwendolyn Cross; Mercy Lewis, Hannah Jo Smith;
           Susanna Walcott, Lois Beckwith; Gustav Meier,
           conductor; Ralph Herbert, stage director.

W55vv.   1983 (June 23, 24): Osaka, Japan; Kohsei-Nenkin
           Hall; Kansai Nikikai Opera Company; Betty
           Parris, Masumi Ohnishi and Masumi Ohnishi;
           Reverend Samuel Parris, Masao Kobayashi and
           Tokihiko Satoh; Tituba, Mika Shigematsu and
           Hiroko Murakami; Abigail Williams, Masako
           Ashihara and Noriko Nishimura; Ann Putnam,
           Kayoko Hamazaki and Eiko Aki; Thomas Putnam,
           Hirozaku Yokota and Makoto Nadai; Rebecca Nurse,

Satoko Yamamoto and Toshiko Kikuchi; Francis
Nurse, Kunitoshi Miyamura and Kiyoshi Kikawada;
Giles Corey, Masaaki Noda; John Proctor,
Hiroyuki Kurata and Tsutomu Masuko; Reverend
John Hale, Seishiroh Okada and Makoto Kikawada;
Elizabeth Proctor, Yoshiko Nire and Kumiko
Okaboh; Mary Warren, Yuko Maruyama and Akiko
Kikui; Ezekiel Cheever, Tadashi Hosokawa and
Kohzoh Urayama; Judge Danforth, Kohdoh Tanaka
and Hiroshi Satoi; Sarah Good, Tomoe Matsui;
Ruth Putnam, Chiaki Takemoto and Yasuko
Kishishita; Martha Sheldon, Ritsuko Miyagi and
Chikako Katsura; Bridget Booth, Yasuko Nakagawa
and Momoko Machida; Mercy Lewis, Akiko Kiriyama
and Michiko Jinno; Susanna Walcott, Nobuko
Sawada and Masako Nomura; Kohtaroh Satoh,
conductor; Kuniaki Hata, stage director.
(Japanese trans. by Kuniaki Hata and Hiroyuki
Kurata) See B158.

W55ww.   1984 (June 5, 6, 8, 9): London; Bloomsbury Theatre;
Abbey Opera; Abigail Williams, Alison
Charlton-West and Alice Hyde; John Proctor,
Alexander Gauld; Reverend John Hale, Stephen
Holloway and Sebastian Swane; Elizabeth Proctor,
Jacqueline Edwards and Amanda Hughes-Jones;
Judge Danforth, Neville Williams and Warwick
Dyer; Antony Shelley, conductor; Paul Hernon,
stage director. See B40, B174.

W55xx.   1985 (May 25-June 2): Chicago; Chicago Opera
Theater; Tituba, Jennifer Jones; Ann Putnam,
Diane Ragains; Rebecca Nurse, Gweneth Bean; John
Proctor, Lawrence Cooper; Elizabeth Proctor,
Cynthia Munzer; Mary Warren, Mary Lagios; Roger
Brunyate, stage director; Mark Flint, conductor.
See B114, B359.

W55yy.   1985 (Aug 17, 18): Seoul, Korea; Sejong Cultural
Center Main Hall; Seoul Opera Group; Korean
Symphony Orchestra; Betty Parris, Kyu-eun Park
and Sun-mi Chung; Reverend Samuel Parris,
Wha-yong Kim and Jung-kyu Lim; Tituba,
Young-soon Kim and You-ree Shon; Abigail
Williams, In-sook Lee and Eun-sook Jung; Ann
Putnam, Ok-ja Kim and Mee-hea-ry Kim; Thomas
Putnam, Chi-ho Yoon and Yo-hun Lie; Rebecca
Nurse, Kyong-aye Lee and Hae-kyung Kang; Francis
Nurse, Young-chan Chun; Giles Corey, Jin-ho Choi
and Se-wan Chang; John Proctor, Soo-kil Park and
Chang-yun Cho; Reverend John Hale, Won-kyung Kim
and Duk-young Han; Elizabeth Proctor, Wha-ja
Kang and Young-ja Chung; Mary Warren, Young-sook
Lee and Ok-hyang Shin; Ezekiel Cheever,
Sang-hoon Lee and Young-moon Kim; Judge
Danforth, Sung-won Park and Hak-su Chong; Sarah
Good, Won-hye Chung and Yeon-seung Lee and
Sun-woo Kim; Ruth Putnam, Mi-kyung Won and

Hyun-joo Chung; Martha Sheldon, Kyung-nyunm Park and Sung-hee Kim; Bridget Booth, Hyun-joo Chung and Ji-eun Kim; Mercy Lewis, In-sook Kim and Mi-ran Choi; Susanna Walcott, Sung-hee Park and Sung-eun Yoo; Robert Ward, conductor; Peter Hogen Moon, stage director. (Korean translation: Ma-nyu sa-nyang) See B186, B349.

W55zz.   1986 (Jan 9, 10, 12): Durham, North Carolina; Bryan University Center, Duke University; Betty Parris, Karen Cummings; Reverend Samuel Parris, Stafford Wing; Tituba, Marietta Simpson; Abigail Williams, Penelope Jensen; Ann Putnam, Loretta Robinson; Thomas Putnam, William Beck; Rebecca Nurse, Deborah Fields; Francis Nurse, Walt Davis; Giles Corey, Patrick Woliver; John Proctor, Steven Kimbrough; Reverend John Hale, Frederic Moses; Elizabeth Proctor, Donna Dease; Mary Warren, Nina Kay Lowe; Ezekiel Cheever, Gerald Postema; Judge Danforth, Mark Jackson; Sarah Good, Loretta Robinson; Ruth Putnam, Marjorie Johnson; Martha Sheldon, Lynn Mae Wilson; Bridget Booth, Judy Hill; Mercy Lewis, Rhoda Chimacoff; Susanna Walcott, Christy Sealy; Robert Ward, conductor; John Clum, stage director. See B195, B292, B356, B361.

W56. HYMN AND CELEBRATION (Feb 28, 1962; revised Mar 1966; Highgate; 10 min.)

For large orchestra
3.2.2.2/4.3.3.1/eh/bcl/timp/perc/hp/str
Commissioned by and dedicated to the Phoenix Symphony and Guy Taylor
Sketches at Duke University
Published: (full score) Highgate, 1969
Hymn section reworked from movement 2 of Two Pieces for the Piano (1941); see W19. Hymn section then reworked into movement 1 of the First String Quartet (1966); see W63.

Premiere

W56a.   1962 (Mar 27): Phoenix, Arizona; Phoenix Union Auditorium; Phoenix Symphony Orchestra; Guy Taylor, conductor. See B152.

Other selected performances

W56b.   1969 (Jan 27, 28): Phoenix, Arizona; Grady Gammage Auditorium (1/27) and Phoenix Union Auditorium (1/28); Phoenix Symphony Orchestra; Guy Taylor, conductor.

W56c.   1969 (July 18): Poggibonsi, Italy; Basilica di S. Lucchese; North Carolina Philharmonic Orchestra;

Gaetano Delogu, conductor.

W56d.   1975 (Nov 21): Winston-Salem, North Carolina; Hanes
          Auditorium, Salem Fine Arts Center; North
          Carolina Symphony; John Gosling, conductor.

W57. NIGHT FANTASY (May 1962; Highgate; 4 min.)

        For concert band
        2.2.3.2/4.0.3.1/picc/ecl/acl/bcl/2asax/tsax/bsax/3ct/
           euph/timp/perc
        Commissioned by Richard Franko Goldman in memory of
           Edwin Franko Goldman
        Sketches at Duke University
        Published: (full and condensed scores, parts)
                   Highgate, 1962

        Premiere

W57a.   1962 (June 20): New York; The Mall, Central Park;
             Goldman Band; Richard Franko Goldman, conductor.

        Other selected performances

W57b.   1963 (July 30): Brevard, North Carolina; Brevard
             Music Center; Transylvania Symphonic Band;
             Richard Franko Goldman, conductor.

W57c.   1968 (May 19): Winston-Salem, North Carolina;
             Reynolds Amphitheater; R.J. Reynolds High School
             Band; Robert Ward, conductor.

W57d.   1968 (July 24): Brooklyn, New York; Music Grove,
             Prospect Park; Goldman Band; Richard Franko
             Goldman, conductor.

W57e.   1968 (July 25): New York; The Mall, Central Park;
             Goldman Band; Richard Franko Goldman, conductor.

W57f.   1972 (Feb 13): Dayton, Ohio; Oakwood High School
             Auditorium; Oakwood High School Band; Frederick
             R. Walker, conductor.

W57g.   1979 (Mar 30): Durham, North Carolina; Baldwin
             Auditorium, Duke University; Duke University
             Wind Symphony; Robert Ward, conductor.

W58. MUSIC FOR A CELEBRATION [TRILOGY FOR ORCHESTRA] (Nov
        1963; withdrawn as such, but see below; 15 min.)

        For orchestra
        3.2.2.2/4.3.3.1/eh/bcl/xyl/timp/perc/str
        Movements: 1. Invocation

> 2. Games and Races
> 3. Processional March
> Commissioned by and dedicated to Broadcast Music,
> Inc., on the occasion of its twentieth anniversary
> Movements 1 and 2 split off in 1966 to form Invocation
> and Toccata; see W67. Movement 3 remains available
> as Processional March; see W59. Movement 3
> reworked into movement 4 of the Fifth Symphony
> (1976); see W73.

Premiere

W58a.   1963 (Nov 19): Erie, Pennsylvania; Memorial
         Auditorium; Erie Philharmonic Orchestra; James
         Sample, conductor. See B12, B47, B89, B128.

W59. PROCESSIONAL MARCH (Nov 1963; Highgate; 6 min.)

> Originally movement 3 of Music for a Celebration
> (1963); for for full information, see W58. This piece
> has remained available from Highgate since movements 1
> and 2 of that piece became Invocation and Toccata in
> 1966; see W67. (See also W73.)

W60. THE LADY FROM COLORADO (July 1964; Highgate; 2 hrs.)

> Opera in two acts
> Minimum cast 12 singers, chorus, corps de ballet
> 2.1.2.1/2.2.2.0/timp/perc/hp/pft/str
> Sketch at Duke University
> Libretto by Bernard Stambler; based on the book by
>   Homer Croy.
> Unpublished; available from Highgate
> Aria "And I hail this bounteous land" (Act II, scene
>   5) reworked from Adventures in Sharps and Flats
>   (c.1955); see W45.

Premiere

W60a.   1964 (July 3, 5, 7, 9, 10, 11, 14, 15, 16, 18, 19,
         21, 23, 24, 25): Central City, Colorado; Central
         City Opera House; Central City Opera House
         Association; Jeff Stafford, John Fiorito and
         Chester Ludgin; Sarah Chicken, Marlena Kleinman
         and Marija Kova and Jean Kraft; Eve St. John,
         Marcia Baldwin and Mignon Dunn; Parson Dowser,
         Michael Ingham; Sister Sunshine, Veryl Berry;
         Tom Wade, Arthur Graham and Richard Krause and
         Mauro Lampi; Maisie Murphy, Matilda Nickel;
         Katie Lawder (Lady Moon), Mary Jennings and Mary
         Ellen Pracht; Jack Spaniard, Raymond Michalsky
         and Thomas Paul; Cecil Moon, Davis Cunningham
         and Thomas Hayward; Rutledge Blunt, Herbert
         Beattie and Lee Cass and Spiro Malas; Mrs. Moon,

Matilda Nickel; Emerson Buckley, conductor;
Christopher West, director; Helen Tamiris,
choreographer. See B37, B121, B216, B237, B238,
B308, B369, B370, B371.

W61. <u>LET THE WORD GO FORTH</u> (Jan 1965; Highgate; 10 min.)

For mixed chorus, with brass, strings, and harp
chorus satb/0.0.0.0/2.2.2.0/str/hp
Alternate version for chorus satb/organ
Text by John F. Kennedy (from Inaugural Address)
Commissioned by and dedicated to the St. Cecilia Club
   and David Buttolph
Sketches (score and text) at Duke University
Unpublished; available from Highgate

Premiere

W61a.   1965 (March 15): New York; Hunter College
           Playhouse; St. Cecilia Society and members of
           the Manhattan School of Music Orchestra; David
           Buttolph, conductor.

W62. <u>SWEET FREEDOM´S SONG: A NEW ENGLAND CHRONICLE</u> (Nov 14,
     1965; Highgate; 40 min.)

Cantata for chorus and orchestra with soprano and
   baritone solos and narrator
solo sopr/solo bass/chorus satb/2.2.2.2/2.2.2.0/timp/
   perc/str/narr
Text compiled by Robert and Mary Ward, from William
   Bradford, Psalm 88, Henry Alford, Anna Barbauld,
   Leonard Bacon, William Tyler Page, James Russell
   Lowell, and Samuel Francis Smith
Movements: 1. Orchestral Prelude
           2. Chorus: It Was a Great Design (Bradford)
           3. Soprano solo: O, Lord God of My
              Salvation (Psalm 88)
           4. Chorus: Come, Ye Thankful People, Come
              (Alford, Barbauld, Bacon)
           5. Chorus: Ballad of Boston Bay
           6. Double chorus: Damnation to the Stamp
              Act
           7. Baritone solo and chorus: Epitaphs
              (Page, Lowell)
           8. Chorus: Let Music Swell the Breeze
              (Smith)
Commissioned by and dedicated to the Lexington Choral
   Society, Allan Lannom, conductor
Sketches at Duke University
Published: (p-v score) Highgate, 1966
           (mvt. 2, p-v score) Highgate, 1965
           (mvt. 7, p-v score) Highgate, 1965

Premiere

W62a.   1965 (Dec 4): Lexington, Massachussetts; Cary Hall;
          Lexington Choral Society; Allan Lannom,
          conductor.

Other selected performances

W62b.   1966 (Dec 29): Washington; Grand Ballroom,
          Mayflower Hotel; Frances Marsh, soprano; Samuel
          Roberson, baritone; Stanley Deacon, narrator;
          Robert Ward, conductor.

W62c.   1967 (Spring): Lawrence, Kansas; University of
          Kansas; Ineta Bebb, soprano; University of
          Kansas Chamber Choir; James Ralston, conductor.

W62d.   1968 (May 21): Winston-Salem, North Carolina; Fine
          Arts Building, Salem College; Clara Allen,
          soprano; John Williams, bass; David Wood,
          narrator; Singer's Guild; David Partington,
          conductor. See B369.

W62e.   1971 (Mar 6): Corpus Christi, Texas; Del Mar
          Auditorium, Del Mar College; Del Mar College
          Choir and selected high-school singers; Del Mar
          Chamber Orchestra; Robert Ward, conductor. See
          B314.

W62f.   1976 (April 6): Winston-Salem, N.C.; R.J. Reynolds
          Memorial Auditorium; Janet Pavek, soprano;
          William Powers, bass-baritone; Franklin R.
          Shirley, narrator; Winston-Salem Symphony
          Orchestra and Chorale; Norman Johnson,
          conductor. See B35, B281, B284, B287.

W62g.   1976 (May 28): Elsah, Illinois; Cox Auditorium,
          Principia College; Robert Balder, narrator; Hale
          Buckingham, reader; Nick Solomon, baritone; Cori
          Weaver, piano; Principia Choir; Robert
          Rockabrand, conductor.

W63. FIRST STRING QUARTET (Mar? 1966; Highgate; 20 min.)

          For string quartet
          Movements: 1. Adagio
                     2. Scherzo
                     3. Allegro marziale
          Dedicated to and commissioned by the University of
             Alabama for the Cadek String Quartet
          Published: (score and parts) Highgate, 1966
          Recorded: Musical Heritage Society, 1979 (D17)
          Movement 2 reworked from movement 1 of Two Pieces for
             the Piano (1941), W19; and Hymn and Celebration

(1962), W56. Movements 2 and 3 reworked into
movements 2 and 4 of <u>Concertino for Strings</u> (1973);
see W71.

Premiere

W63a.   1966 (Apr 30): University, Alabama; Cadek
Conservatory Concert Hall, University of
Alabama; Cadek Quartet; Emil Raab, Michael
Gattozze, violins; Henry Barrett, viola;
Margaret Christy, cello.

Other selected performances

W63b.   1966 (Nov 1): Rochester, New York; Kilbourn Hall,
Eastman School of Music; Cadek Quartet. See
B295.

W63c.   1966 (Nov 5): Location unknown; Cedar Bluff
Elementary School Auditorium; Cadek Quartet.

W63d.   1966 (Nov 6): University, Alabama; Cadek
Conservatory Concert Hall, University of
Alabama; Cadek Quartet.

W63e.   1967 (Jan 9): New York; McMillin Academic Theater;
Paul Zukofsky, Jeanne Benjamin, violins; Jacob
Glick, viola; Robert Sylvester, cello.

W63f.   1967 (Feb 5): Birmingham, Alabama; Hill Hall,
Birmingham-Southern College; Cadek Quartet.

W63g.   1967 (Feb 15): Sweet Briar, West Virginia; Mary
Reynolds Babcock Auditorium, Sweet Briar
College; Cadek Quartet.

W63h.   1967 (Feb 16): Greenville, [South Carolina?];
Greenville County Museum of Art; Cadek Quartet.

W63i.   1967 (Sept 18): Rock Hill, South Carolina; James F.
Byrnes Auditorium, Winthrop College; Cadek
Quartet.

W63j.   1971 (Mar 5): Corpus Christi, Texas; Wolfe Recital
Hall, Del Mar College; Del Mar Faculty String
Quartet; Achille di Russo and Donna Kole,
violins; Lawrence Chidester, viola; Mary Mayhew,
cello. See B314.

W63k.   1980 (May 4): Albany, New York; New York State
Museum; Capitol Chamber Artists; Mary Lou
Saetta, Briget Brodwin, violin; Jacob Glick,
viola; Janet Nepke, cello. See B322.

W64. <u>HYMN TO THE NIGHT</u> (Aug 1966; Highgate; 7 min.)

　　　　For orchestra
　　　　2.2.2.2/4.3.3.1/eh/hp/timp/perc/str
　　　　Tone poem based on the poem by Henry Wadsworth
　　　　　　Longfellow
　　　　Commissioned by Edward B. Benjamin for the Mobile
　　　　　　Symphony Orchestra
　　　　Unpublished; available from Highgate

　　　　<u>Premiere</u>

W64a.　　　1967 (Jan 9): Mobile, Alabama; Mobile Municipal
　　　　　　Theater; Mobile Symphony and Civic Music
　　　　　　Association; James Yestadt, conductor. See B96.

W65. <u>FESTIVE ODE</u> (Sept 1966; Highgate; 11 min.)
　　　　For orchestra
　　　　3.2.2.2/4.3.3.1/eh/bcl/timp/perc/str
　　　　Commissioned by and dedicated to the Milwaukee
　　　　　　Symphony Orchestra, Harry John Brown, conductor.
　　　　Sketches at Duke University
　　　　Published: (full score) Highgate, 1973
　　　　Recorded: Musical Heritage Society, c.1973 (D15).

　　　　<u>Premiere</u>

W65a.　　　1966 (Oct 3): Milwaukee; Pabst Theatre; Milwaukee
　　　　　　Symphony Orchestra; Harry John Brown, conductor.
　　　　　　See B46, B166, B224.

W66. <u>FIESTA PROCESSIONAL</u> (Oct 1966; Highgate; 4.5 min.)

　　　　For concert band
　　　　2.2.3.2/4.2.3.1/picc/eh/ech/acl/bcl/2asax/tsax/
　　　　　　bsax/hp(pft)/3ct/euph/db/timp/perc
　　　　Commissioned by and dedicated to the Ithaca High
　　　　　　School Band, Frank Battisti, conductor
　　　　Published: (full and condensed scores, parts)
　　　　　　　　　　Highgate, 1969

　　　　<u>Premiere</u>

W66a.　　　1967 (May 17): Ithaca, New York; Ford Auditorium,
　　　　　　Ithaca College; Ithaca High School Concert Band;
　　　　　　Frank L. Battisti, conductor.

W67. <u>INVOCATION AND TOCCATA</u> (Dec 1966; Highgate; 9 min.)

　　　　For orchestra
　　　　3.2.2.2/4.3.3.1/eh/bcl/timp/perc/str

Movements: 1. Invocation
            2. Toccata
Commissioned by and dedicated to Broadcast Music,
    Inc., on the occasion of its twentieth anniversary
Sketches at Duke University
Published: (full score) Highgate, 1975
Recorded: Musical Heritage Society, c.1973 (D15)
Originally movements 1 and 2 of Music for a
    Celebration (1963); see W58. Split off to form
    this piece in 1966. See also Processional March
    (1963), W59.

Selected performance

W67a.   1984 (Feb 19): Winston-Salem, N.C.; Hanes Theater,
         North Carolina School of the Arts; NCSA
         Orchestra; Robert Ward, conductor.

W68. ANTIPHONY FOR WINDS (Feb? 1967; Highgate; 5.5 min.)

    For symphonic band or symphonic winds
        3.2.3.2/4.0.3.1/eh/ecl/acl/bcl/2asax/tsax/bsax/3ct/
        euph/db/timp/perc; orchestral version omits
        cl3/acl/asax/tsax/bsax/euph/db
    Commissioned by and dedicated to Jack L. Herriman and
        James Funkhouser for the Youth Symphony of Kansas
        City
    Sketches at Duke University
    Published: (full score and parts) Highgate, 1973

    Premiere

W68a.   1967 (Apr 30): Interlochen, Michigan; National
         Music Camp; Youth Symphony of Kansas City; Jack
         L. Herriman, conductor.

    Other selected performances

W68b.   1967 (May 7): Kansas City; Music Hall; Youth
         Symphony of Kansas City; James Funkhouser,
         conductor.

W68c.   1968 (May 12): Kansas City; Lee's Summit High
         School; Training Orchestra of the Youth Symphony
         of Kansas City; Jack L. Herriman, conductor.

W68d.   1971 (Mar 5): Corpus Christi, Texas; Del Mar
         Auditorium, Del Mar College; Del Mar College
         Wind Ensemble; Richard Kole, conductor. See
         B314.

W68e.   1973 (Dec 9): Stony Brook, N.Y.; Administration
         Building, SUNY-Stony Brook; University Band;
         Simon Karasick, conductor.

W68f.   1979 (Mar 30): Durham, North Carolina; Baldwin

Auditorium, Duke University; Duke University
Wind Symphony; Robert Ward, conductor.

W69. CONCERTO FOR PIANO AND ORCHESTRA (June 1968; Highgate;
30 min.)

For piano and orchestra
pft/3.2.2.2/4.3.3.1/eh/bcl/timp/perc/str
Movements: 1. Adagio--Allegro
2. Grave
Commissioned by the Powder River Foundation for Miss
Marjorie Mitchell
Dedicated to Mrs. Edwin Watson
Published: (2-piano) Highgate, 1970
Recorded: Desto, c.1970 (D14)

Premiere

W69a.   1968 (June 23): Columbia, Maryland; Merriweather
Post Pavilion; Marjorie Mitchell, piano;
Washington National Symphony Orchestra; Howard
Mitchell, conductor. See B153, B189, B205.

Other selected performances

W69b.   1969 (Feb 4): Winston-Salem, North Carolina; R.J.
Reynolds Memorial Auditorium; Marjorie Mitchell,
piano; Winston-Salem Symphony; John Iuele,
conductor. See B180.

W69c.   1979 (Jan 27): Kingsport, Tennessee; Ross N.
Robinson Auditorium; Marjorie Mitchell, piano;
Kingsport Symphony Orchestra; Robert Ward,
conductor. See B296.

W69d.   1984 (Feb 19): Winston-Salem, N.C.; Hanes Theater,
North Carolina School of the Arts; Hyung-Sook
Kim, piano; NCSA Orchestra; Robert Ward,
conductor.

W70. MUSIC FOR A GREAT OCCASION (Sept 25, 1970; withdrawn; 4
min.)

For symphonic band
2.2.3.1/4.0.3.1/picc/eh/ecl/acl/bcl/2asax/tsax/bsax/
3ct/euph/db/timp/perc
Commissioned by Dr. and Mrs. James Semans for the
inauguration of Terry Sanford, fifth president of
Duke University
Unpublished; manuscript at Duke University
Reworked into movement 1 of Four Abstractions for Band
(1977); see W74.

W70a.   1970 (Oct 18): Durham, North Carolina; Main
          Quadrangle, Duke University; Duke University
          Concert Band; Paul Bryan, conductor.

W71. CONCERTINO FOR STRINGS (Spring 1973; Highgate; 15 min.)

          For string orchestra
          2vnI/2vnII/2va/2vc/db
          Movements: 1. Introduction
                     2. Scherzo
                     3. Siciliano
                     4. Allegro Marziale
          Unpublished; available from Highgate
          Movements 2 and 4 reworked from movements 2 and 3 of
            the First String Quartet (1966); see W63. Movement
            3 reworked from movement 4 of Earth Shall Be Fair
            (1960); see W53.

          Premiere

W71a.   1973 (April; May 4) On tour and Winston-Salem,
          North Carolina; Piedmont Chamber Orchestra;
          Nicholas Harsanyi, conductor.

W72. THE PROMISED LAND (ON JORDAN'S STORMY BANKS) (Oct 1974;
      Highgate; 6 min.)

          Chorale prelude for organ or orchestra, with optional
            congregational participation
          2.2.2.2/4.3.3.1/timp/perc/str/congregation ad.lib.
          Alternate version for organ and congregation ad.lib.
          Based on hymn "On Jordan's Stormy Banks" in The
            Baptist Hymnal (Nashville: Convention Press, 1975),
            no. 490
          Text adapted from Samuel Stennett
          Written for and commissioned by the Southern Baptist
            Church and Thor Johnson
          Sketches at Duke University
          Published: (organ version) Highgate, 1977

          Premiere

W72a.   1975 (March 11): Nashville, Tennessee; Municipal
          Auditorium; Nashville Symphony Orchestra;
          Amerigo Marino, conductor.

W73. <u>FIFTH SYMPHONY: CANTICLES OF AMERICA</u> (Apr 2, 1976;
     Highgate; 35 min.)

     For mixed chorus, orchestra, soprano and baritone
         solos, and optional narrator
     chorus satb/solo sopr/solo bar/narr/2.2.2.2/4.3.3.1/
         timp/perc/str
     Text compiled by Robert and Mary Ward; from Walt
         Whitman and Henry Wadsworth Longfellow
     Movements: 1. Behold, America (Whitman)
                2. A Psalm of Life (Longfellow)
                3. Hymn to the Night (Longfellow)
                4. All Peoples of the Globe Together Sail
                   (Whitman)
     Commissioned by and dedicated to the Charlotte
         Oratorio Singers and Conductor, Donald Plott, for
         the celebration of the American Bicentennial.
     Sketches (score and text) at Duke University
     Published: (p-v score) Highgate, 1979.
                (mvt. 2, p-v score) Highgate, 1979.
                (mvt. 3, sopr/vn/pft) Highgate, 1979.
     Movement 4 reworked from <u>Processional March</u> (1963),
         which was itself movement 3 of <u>Music for a</u>
         <u>Celebration</u> (1963); see W58, W59.

     <u>Premiere</u>

W73a.   1976 (May 1): Charlotte, North Carolina; Ovens
         Auditorium; Charlotte Oratorio Singers; Robert
         Horton, narrator; Janice Harsanyi, soprano;
         William Metcalf, baritone; Donald Plott,
         conductor. See B77, B80, B207, B208.

     <u>Other selected performances</u>

W73b.   1976 (May 2): Winston-Salem, North Carolina; Wait
         Chapel, Wake Forest University; same performers
         as premiere. See B280, B285.

W74. <u>FOUR ABSTRACTIONS FOR BAND</u> (Feb? 1977; Highgate; 15
     min.)

     For symphonic band
     2.2.3.2/4.0.3.1/picc/eh/ecl/acl/bcl/2asax/tsax/bsax/
         3ct/euph/db/hp(pft)/timp/perc
     Movements: 1. Jagged Rhythms in Fast Tempo
                2. Color Masses and Luminous Lines in Dark
                   Blue
                3. Curves and Points of Light in Motion
                4. Interweaving Lines
     Commissioned by and dedicated to the Oakwood High
         School Band and its director, Frederick R. Walker
     Sketches at Duke University
     Published: (mvt. 1, full score & parts) Highgate, 1981
                (mvts. 2-3, score & parts) Highgate, 1981

Movement 1 reworked from <u>Music for a Great Occasion</u>
(1970); see W70.

Premiere

W74a.   1977 (May 13): Dayton, Ohio; Oakwood High School
           Band; Frederick R. Walker, conductor.

Other selected performances

W74b.   1984 (Feb 28): Buies Creek, North Carolina; Turner
           Auditorium, Campbell University; Campbell
           University Wind Ensemble; Robert Ward, conductor
           (mvt. 1 only).

W75. <u>CLAUDIA LEGARE</u> (1977; revised June 1978; Highgate; 2
     hrs.)

     Opera in four acts
     Minimum cast 7 singers
     2.2.2.2/4.3.2.0/hp/timp/perc/str; alternate version
        (prepared 1981 by Michael Ching and Robert Ward)
        for cl/hn/pft/str
     Libretto by Bernard Stambler; based on the play <u>Hedda</u>
        <u>Gabler</u> by Henrik Ibsen
     Commissioned by the New York City Opera Company and
        its director, Julius Rudel, under a grant from the
        Ford Foundation
     Sketches (score and libretto) at Duke University
     Published: (libretto) Highgate, 1978

Premiere

W75a.   1978 (April 14, 20, 22): Minneapolis; Guthrie
           Theatre; Minnesota Opera; Aunt Julia Lowndes,
           Susan Chastain; Jennie, Janis Hardy; George
           Lowndes, Vern Sutton; Claudia Legare Lowndes,
           Barbara Brandt; Daphne Grayson, Marsha Hunter;
           Colonel Blagden, Carl Glaum; Orlando Beaumont
           and General Legare, John Brandstetter;
           Carpenters, Dean Benforado and Tim Caris; H.
           Wesley Balk, stage director; Philip Brunelle,
           conductor. See B79, B99, B131, B135, B137, B147.

Other selected performances

W75b.   1981 (July 28): Durham, North Carolina; Fine Arts
           Center Theatre, Durham Academy Upper School;
           Duke University Summer Festival of the Arts
           Theatre Company; Aunt Julia Lowndes, Julie Hull;
           Jennie, Eileen Marie Moore; George Lowndes,
           Michael Best; Claudia Legare Lowndes, Elizabeth
           Pruett; Daphne Grayson, Marsha Andrews; Colonel
           Blagden, William Beck; Orlando Beaumont, David
           Kline; John Clum, stage director; Michael Ching,

conductor. (Chamber version)   See B25, B28,
B71, B145, B211, B246, B247.

W76. <u>CELEBRATIONS OF GOD IN NATURE</u> (Nov 1979; Highgate; 8
min.)

For organ
Movements: 1. The Glorious Sun
           2. The Pensive Moon
           3. The Capricious Wind
Commissioned by the Twin Cities Chapter of the
     American Guild of Organists for the 1980 National
     Convention of the American Guild of Organists
Sketches at Duke University
Published: Highgate, 1980
Movement 2 reworked into movement 1 of the <u>Concerto
for Saxophone and Orchestra</u> (1983); see W81.

<u>Premiere</u>

W76a.   1980 (June 18): St. Paul, Minnesota; Cathedral of
         St. Paul; Robert Glasgow, organ. See B14, B188.

W77. <u>SONIC STRUCTURE</u> (May 1980; Highgate; 11 min.)

For orchestra
3.2.2.2/4.3.3.1/eh/bcl/cbsn/timp/perc/str
Written under a fellowship from the National Endowment
     for the Arts
Dedicated to the Nashville Symphony Orchestra and its
     musical director, Michael Charry, for the opening
     of their first season in the Andrew Jackson Concert
     Hall; also in commemoration of the life of the
     composer´s brother, architect David Ward.
Sketches at Duke University
Unpublished; available from Highgate

<u>Premiere</u>

W77a.   1980 (Sept 25): Nashville, Tennessee; Andrew
         Jackson Concert Hall; Nashville Symphony
         Orchestra; Michael Charry, conductor.

W78. <u>ABELARD AND HELOISE</u> (Dec 1981; revised Mar 1983;
     Highgate; 2 hrs.)

Opera in three acts with prologue
Cast 11 singers, 2 children (non-singing), chorus
2.2.2.2/2.1.1.0/hp/timp/2perc/str
Libretto by Jan Hartman
Commissioned by and dedicated to the Charlotte Opera

Association and its General Director, Richard
Marshall
Sketches at Duke University
Unpublished; available from Highgate

Premiere

W78a.   1982 (Feb 19, 21): Charlotte, North Carolina; Ovens
         Auditorium; Charlotte Opera Association;
         Charlotte Symphony Orchestra; Peter the
         Venerable and Zophar, Timothy Braden; Heloise,
         Nancy Shade; Thibault, William Beck; Job's Wife,
         Berthe, and Prioress, Phyllis Tektonidis; Job
         and Alberic, Harold McIntosh; Eliphaz and
         Lotulf, Stephen Hamilton; Bildad, Mary Lee
         Cooke; Student, Jim Lee; Tradesman and Clerk,
         Michael A. Washington; Tradesman, Andrew
         Steward; Abelard, Jerold Norman; Bernard,
         Malcolm Smith; Fulbert, Vern Sutton; Denys,
         Chester Ludgin; Rhoda Levine, stage director;
         Richard Marshall, conductor. See B2, B41, B92,
         B93, B94, B104, B157, B213, B239, B255, B282,
         B288, B289, B318, B319, B360, B362.

Other selected performances

W78b.   1982 (Jan 28): Durham, North Carolina; Nelson Music
         Room, Duke University; Duke Opera Ensemble; Kathryn
         Huestis, piano; John Hanks, conductor. (Preview of
         Act I, scenes 2-3)

W78c.   1982 (Feb 23): Durham, North Carolina; Page
         Auditorium, Duke University; North Carolina Opera;
         Charlotte Symphony Orchestra; same cast as premiere
         except Buzz Foster replaces Andrew Steward. See
         B3, B4, B5, B141,

W79. <u>MINUTES TILL MIDNIGHT</u> (May 23, 1982; Highgate; 2 hrs.)

Opera in three acts
Minimum cast 5 singers, chorus, dancers
2.2.2.2/4.2.2.0/timp/2perc/hp/str
Libretto by Daniel Lang
Commissioned by Southeast Bank
Dedicated to the people of Dade County [Florida]
Published: (libretto) Highgate, 1982
Theme from an aria reworked into <u>Festival Triptych</u>
    (1986); see W85.

Premiere

W79a.   1982 (June 4, 6, 8, 10): Miami, Florida; Dade
         County Auditorium; Greater Miami Opera; Emil
         Rozak, Thomas Stewart; Chris Jessup, Henry
         Price; Julie Day, Claudia Cummings; Margo

Roszak, Evelyn Lear; Amory Dexter, Richard
Cross; Security Council, Eric Coyne and Keith
Crawford and Albert F. Kunze III and Joel Hume
and Fred Heringes and Daria Trehy Gerwig; Television Newscaster, Ralph Renick; Emerson Buckley, conductor; Nathaniel Merrill, director;
Saeko Ichinohe, choreographer; Gunther Schneid-
er-Siemssen, settings, projections, and
lighting. See B67, B104, B156, B175, B187, B245,
B257, B259, B290, B293, B326, B327, B365, B367.

W80. <u>DIALOGUES FOR VIOLIN, CELLO AND ORCHESTRA</u> (Feb. 1983;
Highgate; 10 min.)

For violin, cello, and orchestra; alternate chamber
version (1984) for violin, cello, and piano; see
W82
solo vn/solo
vc/2.2.2.2/4.3.3.1/eh/bcl/xyl/timp/perc/str
Commissioned by the Chattanooga Symphony
Dedicated to the Chattanooga Symphony Orchestra´s
Fiftieth Anniversary Commemoration, 1982-1983, Dr.
Richard Cormier, Music Director and Conductor
Sketches (both versions) at Duke University
Published (both versions): Highgate, 1986

Premieres

W80a. 1983 (April 5): Chattanooga, Tennessee; Tivoli
Theatre; Donald Zimmer, violin; James Stroud,
cello; Chattanooga Symphony Orchestra; Richard
Cormier, conductor. (orchestral version)

W80b. 1984 (Feb 4): Durham, North Carolina; Nelson Music
Room, Duke University; Claudia Bloom, violin; Fred
Raimi, cello; Randall Love, piano. (chamber
version)

W81. <u>CONCERTO FOR SAXOPHONE AND ORCHESTRA</u> (Feb 1984; revised
summer 1987; Highgate; 18 min.)

For tenor saxophone and orchestra
solo tsax/2.2.2.2/4.3.2.1/picc/eh/bcl/btrb/perc/hp/str
Movements: 1. Lento
           2. [Allegro]
           (Also originally an Allegro movement at the
           beginning)
Dedicated to James Houlik, the Charlotte Symphony and
its conductor, Leo Driehuys; written under a grant
from the National Endowment for the Arts
Sketches at Duke University
Unpublished; available from Highgate
Movement 1 reworked from movement 2 of <u>Celebrations of
God in Nature</u> (1979); see W76. Movement 2 reworked
from <u>Just as You Were</u> (1943); see W26.

Premiere

W81a.   1984 (Feb 15): Charlotte, North Carolina; Ovens
         Auditorium; James Houlik, saxophone; Charlotte
         Symphony; Leo Driehuys, conductor. See B38,
         B198, B240.

W82. DIALOGUES FOR VIOLIN, CELLO & PIANO (Jan 1984)

    Chamber version of Dialogues for Violin, Cello and
       Orchestra (1983); for full information, including
       performances and publication, see W80.

W83.   LAMENTATION AND SCHERZO (1984)

    Publisher's combination of two separately-written
    piano pieces. For fuller information, see Lamentation
    (1946), W30; and Scherzo (1950), W41.

W84. RALEIGH DIVERTIMENTO (Nov 1985; Highgate; 12 min.)

    For wind quintet
    1.1.1.1/1.0.0.0
    Movements: 1. Allegro
               2. Molto adagio
    Commissioned for the Aspen Wind Quintet by the Raleigh
       Chamber Music Guild
    Sketches at Duke University
    Published (score and parts) Highgate, 1986

    Premiere

W84a.   1986 (Jan 19): Raleigh, North Carolina; Steward
         Theater, North Carolina State University; Aspen
         Wind Quintet; Bärli Nugent, flute; Claudia
         Coonce, oboe; David Krakauer, clarinet; Kaitilin
         Mahony, horn; Timothy Ward, bassoon. See B195.

W85. FESTIVAL TRIPTYCH (Jul 1986; Highgate; 14 min.)

    For orchestra and optional narrator
    3.2.2.2/4.3.3.1/eh/bcl/timp/perc/hp/str/narr
    Text by Fred Chappell
    Movements: 1. Adagio
               2. Lento
               3. Vivo
    Commissioned by the Eastern Music Festival

Unpublished; available from Highgate
Movement 1 reworked from <u>Minutes till Midnight</u> (1982);
see W79. Movement 3 reworked from <u>Jonathon and the
Gingery Snare</u> (1949); see W38.

<u>Premiere</u>

W85a.   1986 (Jul 19): Greensboro, North Carolina; Dana
          Auditorium, Guilford College; Johanna Morrison,
          narrator; Eastern Philharmonic Orchestra;
          Sheldon Morgenstern, conductor. See B165.

W86. <u>DIALOGUE ON THE TIDES OF TIME</u> (Apr 1987); Highgate; 8
      min.)

      For solo violin and cello and orchestra or piano
      solo vn/solo vc/2.2.2.2/4.2.0.0/perc/str
      Alternate chamber version vn/vc/pft (being revised at
          press time; may be withdrawn)
      Written for a Memorial Concert for Peace and dedicated
          to Jaime Laredo and Sharon Robinson
      Unpublished; available from Highgate

      <u>Premiere</u>

W86a.   1987 (May 26): Durham, North Carolina; Duke Chapel,
          Duke University; Jaime Laredo, violin; Sharon
          Robinson, cello; Carolina Memorial Concert for
          Peace Symphony Orchestra; Robert Ward,
          conductor. See B194, B324.

LIST OF ABBREVIATIONS

The abbreviations used to give the instrumentation of each
piece are probably more or less self-explanatory. The
standard orchestral woodwinds and brass are expressed (even
for non-orchestral pieces) with numerals; for example, the
indication 2.2.2.2/4.2.2.1 means two flutes, two oboes, two
clarinets, two bassoons, four horns, two trumpets, two
trombones, and one tuba. Other instruments and voice parts
are given with the following system of abbreviations.

```
acl.........alto clarinet
asax.......alto saxophone
bcl.........bass clarinet
bsax...baritone saxophone
btrb........bass trombone
cbcl..contrabass clarinet
cbsn........contrabassoon
cel...............celesta
ct.................cornet
cym...............cymbals
db............double bass
dr..................drums
ecl.......E-flat clarinet
eh..........english horn
euph...........euphonium
hp..................harp
jr................junior
narr............narrator
perc..........percussion
pft................piano
picc.............piccolo
satb........soprano,alto,
              tenor, bass
sax............saxophone
sopr.............soprano
str...strings (ordinarily
         2vn, 2va, vc, db)
timp.............timpani
tpt..............trumpet
trbn...........trombone
tsax......tenor saxophone
va.................viola
vc.................cello
vn................violin
xyl............xylophone
```

PUBLISHER DIRECTORY

Highgate Press
131 West 86th Street
New York, New York 10024

Peer-Southern Organization
1740 Broadway
New York, New York 10019

H.W. Gray
c/o Belwin Mills Publishing Co.
16 West 61st Street
New York, New York 10023

Most unpublished material can be consulted at:

Robert Ward Archive
Music Library, Duke University
6695 College Station
Durham, North Carolina 27708

Discography

This section describes all commercially available recordings, past and present, of Robert Ward's music. Each record (not each piece) receives its own entry, and the entries are presented in chronological order.

Each entry contains the title of the album; the date of its release; the record company and serial number; the performers; the Ward compositions included; and a list of other compositions also on the album. All these are, when possible, cross-referenced with the Works and Performances and Bibliography sections.

As is universally the case in discographies, the album titles are often ambiguous and the dates of release often unknown. Dates in [brackets] should be regarded as hypothetical and approximate.

D1. CONTEMPORARY AMERICAN COMPOSERS [1955] See B53.

Remington R-199-185
Cincinnati Symphony Orchestra; Thor Johnson, conductor
Includes Third Symphony (W39).
Also includes Leon Stein, Three Hassidic Dances.

D2. RECORDINGS OF WORKS COMMISSIONED BY THE LOUISVILLE
     PHILHARMONIC SOCIETY [1955]

Louisville Philharmonic Society LOU-545-10
Louisville Orchestra; Robert Whitney, conductor.
Includes Euphony for Orchestra (W43).

D3. HENRY COWELL: SYMPHONY NO. 7; ROBERT WARD: JUBILATION
     OVERTURE, ADAGIO & ALLEGRO FOR ORCHESTRA [1956]

M-G-M Records E 3084
Vienna Symphony Orchestra; William Strickland,
    conductor.
Includes Adagio and Allegro (W27); Jubilation--An
    Overture (W28).
Also includes Henry Cowell, Symphony No. 7.

D4. CARL RUGGLES: ORGANUM; ROBERT WARD: SYMPHONY NO. 2;
     DOUGLAS MOORE: IN MEMORIAM [1960] See B43.

Composers Recordings CRI SD 127
Japan Philharmonic; William Strickland, conductor (for
Ward and Moore; Akeo Watanabe for Ruggles).
Includes Symphony No. 2 (W31).
Also includes Carl Ruggles, Organum; Douglas Moore, In
Memoriam.

D5. THE CRUCIBLE [1962] See B9, B155, B184, B252, B269.

Composers Recordings CRI 168
New York City Opera; Original cast (see W55a) except
    Tituba, Gloria Wynder; Ann Putnam, Naomi Farr;
    Reverend John Hale, John Macurdy; Mary Warren,
    Nancy Foster; Ezekiel Cheever, Richard Krause;
    Judge Danforth, Jack DeLon; Sarah Good, Naomi Farr;
    Martha Sheldon, Marija Kova; Mercy Lewis, Elizabeth
    Schwering; Emerson Buckley, conductor.
Includes The Crucible (W55).

D6.   ROBERT WARD: JUBILATION OVERTURE; LESTER TRIMBLE:
        CLOSING PIECE; PHILIP BEZANSON: RONDO-PRELUDE; FORREST
        GOODENOUGH: ELEGY [1962]

        Composers Recordings CRI 159
        Vienna Symphony Orchestra; William Strickland,
            conductor (for Ward; other orchestras for other
            pieces).
        Includes Jubilation--An Overture (W28).
        Also includes Lester Trimble, Closing Piece; Philip
            Bezanson, Rondo-Prelude; Forrest Goodenough, Elegy
            for Orchestra.

D7.   HENRY COWELL: ...IF HE PLEASE; ROBERT WARD: HUSH'D BE
        THE CAMPS TODAY; LEO SOWERBY: CLASSIC CONCERTO FOR
        ORGAN AND STRING ORCHESTRA [1963]

        Composers Recordings CRI 165
        Norwegian Choir of Solosingers; Rolf Karlsen, organ;
            Members of the Oslo Philharmonic Orchestra; William
            Strickland, conductor.
        Includes Hush'd Be the Camps Today (W12).
        Also includes Henry Cowell, ...If He Please; Leo
            Sowerby, Classic Concerto for Organ and String
            Orchestra.

D8.   SONGS BY AMERICAN COMPOSERS [1963]

        Originally St/And SPL 411/412; then [1964] Desto D
            411/412 (mono), DST 6411-6412
        John McCollum, baritone; Edwin Biltcliffe, piano (for
            Ward; other singers and pianists for other pieces)
        Includes Sorrow of Mydath (W9).
        Also includes 4 songs by Tennessee Williams; 3 songs
            each by Otto Luening, John Gruen; 2 songs each by
            David Diamond, Irving Fine, William Flanagan,
            Douglas Moore, Theodore Chanler; 1 song each by
            Vincent Persichetti, Ned Rorem, Charles Ives, Jack
            Beeson, William Bergsma, Charles T. Griffes, John
            LaMontaine, Virgil Thomson, Edward MacDowell, Aaron
            Copland, Daniel Pinkham, Ben Weber, Henry Cowell.

D9.   ROBERT WARD: DIVERTIMENTO; JACOB AVSHALOMOV: PHASES OF
        THE GREAT LAND [1964]

        Composers Recordings CRI 194
        Portland Junior Symphony; Jacob Avshalomov, conductor.
        Includes Divertimento for Orchestra (W54).
        Also includes Jacob Avshalomov, Phases of the Great
            Land.

D10. VIRGIL THOMSON: SUITE FROM "THE RIVER"; ROBERT WARD:
      SYMPHONY NO. 1 [1964]

      Desto D-405 (Mono), DST-6405 (Stereo)
      Vienna Symphony Orchestra; Dean Dixon, conductor (for
         Ward; Walter Hendl for Thomson).
      Includes the First Symphony (W16).
      Also includes Virgil Thomson: Suite from "The River".

D11. CONCERTO FOR PIANO AND ORCHESTRA BY ALEXEI HAIEFF;
      SYMPHONY #1 BY ROBERT WARD [c1964]

      American Recording Society ARS-19
      American Recording Society Orchestra; Dean Dixon,
         conductor (for Ward; Walter Hendl for Haieff)
      Includes Symphony No. 1 (W16)
      Also includes Alexei Haieff, Concerto for Piano and
         Orchestra.

D12. ROBERT WARD: SACRED SONGS FOR PANTHEISTS; SYMPHONY NO.
      3 [1966]

      Composers Recordings CRI-206
      (1) Iceland Symphony Orchestra; Igor Buketoff,
         conductor; (2) Sylvia Stahlman, soprano; Polish
         National Radio Orchestra; William Strickland,
         conductor.
      Includes (1) Third Symphony (W39); (2) Sacred Songs
         for Pantheists (W42).

D13. EDUCATIONAL RECORD REFERENCE LIBRARY, BAND PROGRAM,
      VOL. 1 (1967)

      Franco Columbo BP-101
      High School Symphonic Band of the National Music Camp
         and Interlochen Arts Academy; Kenneth Snapp,
         conductor (for Ward; other bands for other pieces).
      Includes band version of Prairie Overture (W51).
      Also includes Vaclav Nelhybel, Symphonic Movement;
         Peter Mennin, Canzona; John Barnes Chance,
         Variations on a Korean Folk Song; Norman Dello
         Joio, Variants on a Mediaeval Tune.

D14. QUINCY PORTER: NEW ENGLAND EPISODES FOR ORCHESTRA;
      ROBERT WARD: CONCERTO FOR PIANO AND ORCHESTRA [c1970]

      Desto DC-7123
      Marjorie Mitchell, piano; Stuttgart Radio Orchestra;
         William Strickland, conductor (for Ward; Polish
         National Radio Orchestra, Vodhan Wodiczko,
         conductor, for Porter).
      Includes Concerto for Piano and Orchestra (W69).

Also includes Quincy Porter, <u>New England Episodes</u>.

D15. <u>ROBERT WARD: PRAIRIE OVERTURE, FANTASIA FOR BRASS CHOIR</u>
      <u>AND TYMPANI, INVOCATION AND TOCCATA, FESTIVE ODE</u>
      [1973]

      Musical Heritage Society MHS 1600
      Polish Radio Orchestra; Bodhan Wodiczko and Zdzislav
        Szostak, conductors.
      Includes <u>Prairie Overture</u> (W51); <u>Fantasia for Brass</u>
        <u>Choir and Timpani</u> (W47); <u>Invocation and Toccata</u>
        (W67); <u>Festive Ode</u> (W65).

D16. <u>NINE SONGS BY CHARLES IVES; SONGS BY THEODORE CHANLER,</u>
      <u>NORMAN DELLO JOIO, IRVING FINE, ROBERT WARD</u> (1977)

      New World Records NW 300
      William Parker, baritone; Dalton Baldwin, piano; Ani
        Kavafian, violin.
      Includes <u>Ballad from Pantaloon</u> (see W46).
      Also includes 9 songs by Charles Ives; 3 songs by
        Theodore Chanler; 1 song by Norman Dello Joio; 4
        songs by Irving Fine.

D17. <u>ROBERT WARD: CHAMBER MUSIC</u> (1979)

      Musical Heritage Society MHS 4138
      (1) Razoumovsky Quartet; Elaine Richey and David
        Moskovitz, violins; Sally Peck, viola; Robert
        Marsh, cello; (2) Mark Ward, cello; Margo Garrett,
        piano; (3) Vartan Manoogian, violin; Anne Epperson,
        piano.
      Includes (1) <u>First String Quartet</u> (W63); (2) <u>Arioso</u>
      <u>and Tarantelle</u> (W44); (3) <u>First Sonata for Violin and</u>
      <u>Piano</u> (W40).

D18. As this volume goes to press, a new recording,
        including <u>Jubilation -- An Overture</u> (W28), the <u>Fourth</u>
      <u>Symphony</u> (W52), the <u>Concerto for Saxophone and</u>
      <u>Orchestra</u> (W81), and <u>Sonic Structure</u> (W77), performed
        by the North Carolina Symphony directed by Gerhardt
        Zimmermann, is being prepared by American Orchestras
        International.

Bibliography

This bibliography of articles by and about Robert Ward is arranged in alphabetical order according to usual bibliographic practice. Each entry is provided with a brief annotation, and items of criticism have, whenever possible, an excerpt to give the general flavor of the review. References in parenthesis (e.g., W29, W56a, or D9) are to pieces, specific performances, and recordings in the Works and Discography sections.

The bibliography is drawn from a wide variety of sources, but it was originally and is substantially based on the collection of clippings and photocopies in the composer´s papers at Duke University. Unfortunately, many of the items in this collection are preserved without full bibliographic information, and such information, particularly for small-town papers around the country, has often proven difficult or impossible to restore. Thus, a few entries here are presented with incomplete or conjectural citations, and the curious reader is encouraged to dig further. All articles in the collection at Duke have been included here, apart from a number of critically or historically uninformative items (e.g., advertisements or simple announcements) and a handful of clippings so fragmentary that no real sense could be made of them.

Readers wishing to read the composer´s own words are directed to the entries under his name and to the list of interviews at the end of the bibliography.

B1.   A., M.T.   "Philharmonic Concert Gets Warm Reception."
      Erie (Pa.) Morning News, November 19, 1958.

          Review of a performance of the First Symphony by
          the Erie Philharmonic Society (W16d). "It is the
          kind of contemporary work that will be played
          repeatedly. To quote the composer, it was not
          alarmingly ´modern´ but its scoring, meaningful and
          well crafted, with its moments of musical
          excitement is virile in mood."

B2.   Abernethy, Martha.   "´Abelard and Heloise´." Raleigh
      (N.C.) Spectator, c.March 1, 1982.

          Review of the premiere of Abelard and Heloise
          (W78c). "Robert Ward´s opera succeeds because he
          sticks mainly to conversational middle registers,
          and because he crafts the music so well that no one
          element of singing, orchestral accompaniment, etc.,
          overpowers any other elements of plot,
          characterization or staging."

B3.   Adams, Allison.   "´Abelard and Heloise´ at Duke." Durham
      (N.C.) Sun, March 11, 1982.

          Review of a performance of Abelard and Heloise by
          the North Carolina Opera in Durham (W78c). "Both
          music and libretto were accessible and appealing."

B4.   Adams, Allison.   "A 12th Century Romance Is Now a New
      Opera," and "Preview of New Opera," Durham (N.C.)
      Sun, February 11, 1982.

          Previews of a performance of Abelard and Heloise in
          Durham (W78c).

B5.   Alexander, Jean.   "Ward Opera Premiere at Cedar Lane
      Stage." Montgomery County (Md.) Sentinel, May 24,
      1979.

          Review of a performance of He Who Gets Slapped by
          the Cedar Lane Stage (W46f). "Ward´s score, though
          modern in character, is tuneful and easy to listen
          to, and the young professional singers ... have
          both the technique and vocal maturity to do full
          justice to Ward´s score."

B6.   Anthony, Michael.   "Opera: ´The Crucible´." Minneapolis
      Tribune, June 22, 1973.

          Review of a performance of The Crucible by the St.
          Paul Opera (W55jj). "Ward´s score is a near-match
          for the dramatic weight of Miller´s play. Though
          occasionally dissonant, the score is anything but

avant-garde. It is continually expressive,
however, passionate, and melodramatic in the way
that Miller's play is melodramatic. There are
touches of 'Pelleas' here, some hymn tunes and even
of Gershwin ..."

B7.   Apone, Carl. "Composer 'In the Spirit'." Pittsburgh
      Press, January 25, 1976.

      Preview of a performance of The Crucible by the
      Pittsburgh Opera (W55qq), with an interview with
      the composer.

B8.   Apone, Carl. "Composer Loses Much of Singing in
      Orchestral Sounds at Heinz Hall." Pittsburgh Press,
      January 30, 1976.

      Review of a performance of The Crucible by the
      Pittsburgh Opera (W55qq). "World's [sic] music is
      honest, fresh and imaginative. The compactness,
      discipline and craftsmanship of his orchestrating
      is most apparent. He is a knowledgeable composer
      totally without any high-flown avant-garde
      posturing. This is the kind of solid, valuable,
      thoughtful music which has reaped a great harvest
      in the past, and seems likely to continue to do so
      in the future."

B9.   Ardoin, John. "'The Crucible' on Discs." Musical
      America 83, no. 2 (February 1963): 39.

      Review of the recording of The Crucible (D5). "...
      Ward's voice is not dominant, and he seems to have
      many questions to resolve in coming to grips with
      the operatic form."

B10. B., R. "Vier neue amerikanische Opern."
      Schweitzerische Musikzeitung 102 (1962): 40-41.

      Review of the premiere of The Crucible (W55aa).
      "Die rühmliche ausnahme bildet Ward, der bei aller
      Konse-quenz, von modischen Extravaganzen
      freizubleiben, ein musikalisches Idiom getroffen
      hat, das eigengesichtige Züge aufweist und
      individuelle Sprache spricht; die Partitur, die fur
      grosse Kammerorchester-Besetzung geschrieben ist,
      frappiert nicht als Meisterwerk sondern durch die
      latenten und effektsicheren Stimmungkontraste, die
      gekonnte Ensembletechnik ... und die gewaltige
      Verdichtung der Aktschlüsse."

B11. Baldwin, Nick. "Compelling S.U.I Opera in 'Crucible'."
      Des Moines (Iowa) Register, August 2, 1962.

      Review of a performance of The Crucible at the
      State University of Iowa (W55d). "... a score
      sufficiently dramatic to do justice to the original
      without diluting the impact of the play."

B12. Barr, Hugh D. "Pianist, Composer, ´Gremlin´ Highlight
      Orchestra Concert." <u>Erie (Pa.) Morning News</u>,
      November 20, 1963.

      Review of the premiere of <u>Music for a Celebration</u>
      (W58a). "The just-completed three-movement work had
      meat and potatoes in the form of flowing
      construction, and classically-oriented ideas for a
      contemporary composition."

B13. Bell, Eleanor. "Paganini Concerto Played." <u>Cincinnati
      Post</u>, April 4, 1954.

      Review of a performance of the <u>Third Symphony</u> by
      the Cincinnati Symphony Orchestra (W39c). "... a
      romantic-sounding work in three movements in which
      I detected little that was original or fresh. Mr.
      Ward ... knows his way about the orchestra and is
      not afraid of tunes, but the symphony struck me as
      being rather shapeless and if it had a point it was
      not made very forcefully."

B14. Belt, Byron. "AGO/80 -- Twin Cities Convention."
      <u>American Organist</u> 14, no. 8 (August 1980): 24-29.

      Review of the premiere of <u>Celebrations of God in
      Nature</u> (W76a). "My scribbled notes described it as
      ´wildly conservative,´ and a friend noted that it
      was the popular opera composer´s first organ
      commission, and hoped that it would be the last."

B15. Biancolli, Louis. "´He Who Gets Slapped´ Presented at
      City Center." <u>New York World-Telegram and Sun</u>,
      April 13, 1959.

      Review of a performance of <u>He Who Gets Slapped</u> by
      the New York City Opera Company (W46b). "The
      orchestral commentary is always alive and helpful
      in the general momentum, and Mr. Ward and his
      librettist, Bernard Stambler -- know how to face
      dramatic crisis without flinching. This opera has
      guts.... From whatever angle, ´He Who Gets
      Slapped´ is a proud American achievement."

B16. Biancolli, Louis. "Ward Opera Debuts at the City
      Center." <u>New York World-Telegram and Sun</u>, October
      27, 1961.

      Review of the premiere of <u>The Crucible</u> (W55a).
      "What Mr. Ward has added is a third dimension that
      can only be supplied by a viable and thrusting
      score. Mr. Miller´s ´The Crucible´ has become a
      still more excoriating indictment in the opera
      based on it. That Mr. Ward does by using the
      singing voice and orchestra to sharpen and amplify
      the mounting mood of frenzied suspicion and
      superstition."

B17.   Biancolli, Louis. "Ward's 4th Offered at Carnegie
        Concert." New York World-Telegram and Sun, March
        18, 1959.

        Review of a performance of the Fourth Symphony by
        the National Orchestral Association (W52b). "Like
        the opera [He Who Gets Slapped], the score shows
        good craftsmanship. The counterpoint is neat, the
        writing clean and facile, too facile. Unlike the
        opera, the symphony lacks the bite of true
        originality."

B18.   "Big Book, Big Song." Time 78, no. 18 (November 3,
        1961): 34-36.

        Review of the premiere of The Crucible (W55a).
        "The main strength of the score is in the vocal
        parts -- vigorous, resourceful, utilizing melody as
        a dramatic weapon.

B19.   Blade, Joe. "St. Paul's 'Crucible' 'Enchants' Reviewer
        Second Time Around." Minneapolis Star, June 22,
        1973.

        Review of a performance of The Crucible by the St.
        Paul Opera (W55jj). "This is not the harsh
        dissonance of clashing chords, though, but an
        appropriate musical development of the disturbing
        story. For those willing to listen beyond the lack
        of singable, Verdi-like melodies, I recommend 'The
        Crucible' most highly."

B20.   Bloch, Henry. [untitled review] Notes 21 (1963-4):
        230-231.

        Review of The Crucible (W55). "It frankly and
        successfully combines traditional elements with a
        contemporary idiom and is deserving of revivals by
        companies whose resources are sufficient to mount a
        large scale production."

B21.   Bloomfield, Arthur. [untitled review] Opera 16 (1965):
        642.

        Review of a performance of The Crucible by the San
        Francisco Opera (W55o). "The music -- nestling
        comfortably between Wagner and Broadway -- could
        pack more tension, display more variety of texture
        and pace."

B22.   Bogart, Jeffrey D. "'Crucible' Opens Season of Opera."
        Kansas City Times, September 18, 1968.

        News story about the opening of a performance of
        The Crucible by the Kansas City Lyric Theater
        (W55x).

B23. Boros, Ethel. "Karamu Opera Gives Lyric Theater
      Boost." <u>Cleveland Plain Dealer</u>, June 1, 1961.

      Review of a performance of <u>He Who Gets Slapped</u> by
      the Karamu Theatre (W46c). "Ward´s music is modern,
      but conservatively so. One need not strain very
      hard to hear how melodious it is, even without an
      orchestra. The vocal lines are graceful and give
      the singers no great difficulty. Of drama there is
      plenty, for this is an opera full of emotions."

B24. Boros, Ethel. "Pianist Fleisher Adds Merit to
      Concert." <u>Cleveland Plain Dealer</u>, October 19, 1962.

      Review of a performance of <u>Euphony for Orchestra</u> by
      the Cleveland Orchestra (W43f). "... it is indeed
      euphonics [sic], easy on the ears, easily under-
      stood. It reflects Ward´s interest in things
      American, notably jazz, and sometimes displays the
      kind of vague, innocuous passion of a Hollywood
      movie soundtrack."

B25. Boswell, Carl. "´Claudia LeGare [sic] a Theater Must."
      <u>Durham (N.C.) Sun</u>, July 28, 1981.

      Review of a performance of <u>Claudia Legare</u> in Durham
      (W75b). "At Rare Moments the music ... threatens
      to dominate the action. But this is so rare it is
      hardly worth mention."

B26. Boulware, Jane. "Premiere Performance for Cantata
      Here." <u>Des Moines Tribune</u>, November 19, 1960.

      Preview of the premiere of <u>Earth Shall Be Fair</u>
      (W53a), with a short interview with the composer.

B27. Boutwell, William D., Burleson, Derek L., and Hunt,
      Loretta E. "Humanities in Action -- at the North
      Carolina School of the Arts." <u>Senior Scholastic</u> 92,
      no. 7 (March 21, 1968): supplement 6-7, 22.

      Interview with Ward about his work at the North
      Carolina School of the Arts.

B28. Broili, Susan. "Claudia LeGare [sic] -- A New Kind of
      Opera." <u>Durham (N.C.) Sun</u>, July 23, 1981.

      Preview of a performance of <u>Claudia Legare</u> in
      Durham (W75b).

B29. Brown, Ray. "Piston´s New Symphony in Washington."
      <u>Modern Music</u> 21 (1944): 179-180.

      Review of a performance of the <u>First Symphony</u> (W16)
      in Washington: "... remarkably mature and
      confident. There is intellectual power in this
      work, expressed with alternate austerity and poetic
      imagination. The first movement has an elemental

force rarely felt in young composers; the andante
is nocturnal in mood,and the scherzo-finale has a
breezy motivation."

B30. Brunn, Josephine. "´The Crucible´ Relives Our
      History." Miami Beach (Fla.) Sun-Reporter, March
      13, 1974.

      Review of a performance of The Crucible by the
      Greater Miami International Opera (W55ll). "Perhaps
      because of its newness, but there isn´t a single
      aria in ´The Crucible´ that you will remember or
      lingers with you as you walk out, but in place of
      mellifluous, romantic melody, you will take instead
      a part of early Americana, the puritans´ haunting
      and unforgettable lesson in stirring chorus, a
      powerfully memorable lesson unequaled by the
      score."

B31. Bush, Geoffrey. "´The Crucible´ Sung by N.E.
      Conservatory." Boston Herald, February 15, 1963.

      Review of a performance of The Crucible at the New
      England Conservatory of Music (W55f). "It was a
      fine play. It is a finer opera, moving more
      quickly and expressing itself more strongly -- it
      is as if music was [what] it always needed."

B32. Campbell, Frank C. "Kindler Foundation Concert
      Presents New Ward Work." Washington Evening Star,
      January 11, 1955.

      Review of the premiere of Arioso and Tarantelle
      (W44a). "In Mr. Ward´s music there are few attempts
      at drastic experiment or soul-searching profundity.
      There is smooth, accomplished craftsmanship in the
      mechanics of the writing, and the music unfolds
      with a lyric flow and naturalness that many an
      innovator might envy."

B33. Cariaga, Daniel. "A Masterful Work." Long Beach (Cal.)
      Independent and Press-Telegram, April 17, 1970.

      Review of a performance of The Crucible at
      California State University at Long Beach (W55z).
      "Robert Ward´s opera, ´The Crucible´ (1961) ... is
      an important and masterful work. The CSLB
      production, seen at it opening, Wednesday night,
      does it justice."

B34. Carman, Judith Elaine. "A Comprehensive Performance
      Project in Solo Vocal Literature with an Essay:
      Twentieth-Century American Song Cycles: A Study in
      Circle Imagery." DMA dissertation, University of
      Iowa, 1973.

      Discussion of circular aspects of, and circle
      imagery in, selected works by American twentieth-

century composers, including unspecified works by
Ward. (See abstract in <u>Dissertation Abstracts
International</u> 35:493A-494A.)

B35. Carr, Genie. "Both Objectivity and Subjectivity."
<u>Winston-Salem (N.C.) Sentinel</u>, April 1, 1976.

Interview with Robert and Mary Ward about their
collaboration on <u>Sweet Freedom's Song</u>; on the
occasion of a performance of the work by the
Winston-Salem Symphony and Chorale (W62f).

B36. Carroll, J. Robert. "Toledo Opera's 'The Crucible'
Proves Moving Musical, Theatrical Treat." <u>Toledo
(Ohio) Times</u>, January 25, 1971.

Review of a performance of <u>The Crucible</u> by the
Toledo Opera Association (W55cc). "The style is
firmly rooted in traditional idioms, but Mr. Ward's
great talent has enabled him to integrate whatever
20th-century developments have appealed to him
without any trace of forcing or awkwardness. A
more sincere and honest musical credo could not be
found among the composers of today or yesterday."

B37. Chapin, Louis. "Ward's 'Lady' in Central City Debut."
<u>Christian Science Monitor</u>, July 8, 1964.

Review of the premiere of <u>The Lady from Colorado</u>
(W60a). "Though the influences of Richard Rodgers
and Aaron Copland figured importantly, Mr. Ward
showed at times his own inventive richness,
especially in orchestration and in choral
writing..."

B38. "Charlotte Symphony Premieres New Work by Robert Ward."
<u>Durham (N.C.) Sun</u>, February 9, 1984.

Preview of the premiere of the <u>Concerto for
Saxophone</u> (W81a), with a short interview with the
composer.

B39. Clark, J. Bunker. "On Stage at KU." <u>Lawrence (Kan.)
Daily Journal-World</u>, May 3, 1967.

Review of a performance of <u>Divertimento</u> by the
Symposium of Contemporary American Music Orchestra
(W54b). "... 'Divertimento' was the climax fo the
evening. The style of the work would be attractive
to a typical concert audience, since it included
strong key centers and even occasional familiar
chord progressions."

B40. Clements, Andrew. [untitled review] <u>Opera</u> 35 (1984):
1043-1044.

Review of a performance of <u>The Crucible</u> by the
Abbey Opera (W55ww). "... while Ward deploys his

musical resources with tact and some sensitivity,
he fails at any point to find an appropriate
instrumental or expressive analogue to the highly
charged atmosphere of the stage drama."

B41. Cofield, Terrell. "Abelard and Heloise by Robert Ward:
      A Viewpoint." Opera Journal 15, no. 3 (1982):
      29-33.

      Review of the premiere of Abelard and Heloise
      (W78a). "There were some moments in the opera that
      needed heightened tension ... But there were many
      more moments of absorbing musical drama, rewarding
      to the audience."

B42. Cohn, Arthur. "Rogers, Diamond and Others and
     Rochester." Modern Music 19 (1942): 267-270.

      Review of a number of recent performances of modern
      music, including the First Symphony (W16a) and
      Hush'd Be the Camps Today (W12a). "Withoug
      choosing to be too severe I still wonder at the
      technical incompetence of Robert Ward's Symphony
      Number 1 with its tonality concept so constricted
      that nothing results, especially in the second
      movement; and the patchy William Walton - Vaughan
      Williams attributes of the final portion.... As a
      balance, however, there was ... the elegiac chorus
      of Hush'd Be the Camps Today of Robert Ward. This
      latter piece has artful voice writing, and is
      nicely incisive in its softness."

B43. C[ohn], A[rthur]. [untitled review] American Record
     Guide 26 (1960): 999.

      Review of the recording of Symphony No. 2 (D4).
      "The Symphony may have Shostakovitch touches ...,
      but it registers well and with considerable effect.
      The factor of consonantial structure with a
      dissonantial façade describes his three-movement
      piece. It is good listening; it is worth owning."

B44. Commanday, Robert. "A Superb Staging of 'The
      Crucible'." San Francisco Chronicle, June 24,
      1965.

      Review of a performance of The Crucible by the San
      Francisco Opera (W55o). "Ward's musical language
      has an immediate appeal that will endear it to
      those who are forever wanting to go away singing
      the tunes.... [T]he trouble with this is that the
      style of the musical, and Ward's language, do not
      contain the resources for dramatic development over
      the long pull."

B45. Commander, Doris. [untitled review] Violins and
      Violinists Magazine 13 (1952): 140.

Review of the <u>First Sonata for Violin and Piano</u>
(W40). "... a sonata of lasting musical worth,
reflecting real inspiration."

B46. "Composer Listens, Frowns and Smiles," <u>Milwaukee
Journal</u>, October 2, 1966.

Preview of premiere of <u>Festive Ode</u> (W65a), with a
short interview with the composer.

B47. "Composer Recalls War Campaigns." <u>Erie (Pa.) Times</u>,
November 18, 1963.

Interview with the composer on the occasion of the
premiere of <u>Music for a Celebration</u> (W58a).

B48. "Composer to Join Duke Staff." <u>Durham (N.C.) Sun</u>,
April 25, 1979.

News story, with a short interview, on Ward's
joining the faculty of Duke University.

B49. "Composer Will Hear Debut of His Opera." <u>Schenectady
(N.Y.) Union-Star</u>, August 16, 1966.

Preview of a performance of <u>The Crucible</u> by the
Lake George Opera Company (W55p).

B50. "Composers in Focus." <u>BMI: The Many Worlds of Music</u>,
Winter 1976: 16-33.

Profiles of the twenty BMI composers most
frequently performed during the 1974-1975 concert
season; biography and interview of Ward on pp.
32-33.

B51. "The Concert Hall." <u>American Composers Alliance
Bulletin</u>:
      2, no. 1 (February 1952): 13-17.
      2, no. 2 (June 1952): 20-24.
      3, no. 4 (Winter 1953-4): 11-16.
      4, no. 1 (1954): 20-26.
      4, no. 2 (1954): 12-13.
      4, no. 4 (1955): 15-21.
      5, no. 2 (1955): 18-24.
      6, no. 1 (Autumn 1956): 14-21.
      7, no. 2 (1958): 23-24.
      7, no. 3 (1958): 18-26.
      7, no. 4 (1958): 22-29.
      8, no. 1 (1958): 21-32.
      8, no. 2 (1959): 21-25.
      8, no. 3 (1959): 20-25.
      8, no. 4 (1959): 22-32.
      9, no. 1 (1959): 19-25.
      9, no. 2 (1960): 18-24.
      9, no. 3 (1960): 26-36.
      9, no. 4 (1961): 19-28.
     10, no. 1 (1962): 19-32.

10, no. 3 (September 1962): 17-35.
11, no. 2-4 (December 1963): 30-44.
12, no. 1 (Spring 1964): 16-24.

Lists performances of Ward's works around the
world, sometimes with critical excerpts. Includes
many performances not listed in the Works section
of this book.

B52. "Concert Music." BMI: The Many Worlds of Music, April
      1967: 12.

      Announcement of Ward's appointment at the North
      Carolina School of the Arts.

B53. Cone, Edward T. "Ward: Symphony No. Three; Stein,
      Three Hassidic Dances." Musical Quarterly 42
      (1956): 423-425.

      Review of the first recording of Symphony No. 3
      (D1). "It is unfortunate that Robert Ward's Third
      Symphony does not measure up to its opening. Yet
      in a way its failures are more interesting than its
      successes, which are for the most part conventional
      and unexciting: the orchestration is lucid and
      slick, and the over-all formal patterns are clear
      and coherent."

B54. Cramer, Roger. "Significant Changes When 'Crucible
      Became Opera." Urbana (Ill.) News-Gazette, November
      12, 1971.

      Preview of a performance of The Crucible at the
      University of Illinois (W55ff), with an interview
      with the composer.

B55. Croan, Robert. "Ward Logical Choice." Pittsburgh
      Post-Gazette, January 27, 1976.

      Preview of a performance of The Crucible by the
      Pittsburgh Opera (W55qq), with an interview with
      the composer.

B56. Croan, Robert. [untitled review] Opera News 40, no.
      19 (April 10, 1976): 30.

      Review of a performance of The Crucible by the
      Pittsburgh Opera (W55qq). "Ward's efficient baton
      technique and sensitivity to instrumental detail
      made him a convincing exponent of his own work..."

B57. "'Crucible' Opens in Macbride Tonight." Iowa City
      (Iowa) Daily Iowan, July 31, 1962.

      Preview of a performance of The Crucible at the
      State University of Iowa (W55d).

B58. "The Crucible: Robert Ward." American Composers

Alliance Bulletin 10, no. 2 (May 1962): 6-10.

Digest of critical commentary on the premiere of
The Crucible (W55a).

B59. Cumming, Robert. "Schanzers Create Admirable
      'Crucible'." Chautauqua (N.Y.) Daily, August 2,
      1976.

      Review of a performance of The Crucible by the
      Chautauqua Opera Association (W55tt). "... the
      music is taut, terrorized, masculine, dignified.
      It has romantic sweep."

B60. Cunningham, Carl. "'Crucible' Ready for First Test."
      Houston (Tex.) Post, February 13, 1972.

      Preview of a performance of The Crucible by the
      Houston Baptist College Opera Company (W55gg).

B61. Cunningham, Carl. "Ward's 'Crucible' Brings Him Here."
      Houston (Tex.) Post, February 18, 1972.

      Interview with the composer on the occasion of a
      performance of The Crucible by the Houston Baptist
      College Opera Company (W55gg).

B62. Cunningham, Carl. "Ward's 'Crucible' in Strong
      Opening." Houston (Tex.) Post, February 9, 1972.

      Review of a performance of The Crucible by the
      Houston Baptist College Opera Company (W55gg).
      "Amazing Bill Guthrie has done it again. Building
      on the merits of [his] 'Marriage of Figaro' ...
      last season, Guthrie and colleagues came up with an
      even more impressive opening of Robert Ward's 'The
      Crucible'..."

B63. Dahl, Ingolf. [untitled review] Notes 15 (1958):
      260-261.

      Review of the Fantasia for Brass Choir and Tympani
      (W47). "The over-all character is rather more
      lyrical than martial and in the last sections the
      rhythmic drive is softened, if not actually
      negated, by the presence of sustained parts."

B64. Dalton, Sydney. "City Symphony Presents Top Radio
      Program." Nashville (Tenn.) Banner [?], c.January
      24, 1949.

      Review of a broadcast of Symphony No. 2 by the
      Nashville Symphony Orchestra (W31c). "The Ward
      Symphony proved to be a definitely original
      exciting and forceful work..."

B65. Dalton, Sydney. "Concert Hailed as Memorable Musical
      Event." Nashville (Tennessee) Banner [?], c.January

26, 1949.

Review of a performance of <u>Symphony No. 2</u> by the
Nashville Symphony Orchestra (W31c)."Between the
rugged vitality of the first and last movement, the
lyricism and melodic freshness of the second
movement are sufficient alone to mark the composer
as something more than a mere technician."

B66. Darack, Arthur. "Francescatti Has the Leading Role."
<u>Cincinnati Enquirer</u>, April 3, 1954.

Review of a performance of the <u>Third Symphony</u> by
the Cincinnati Symphony Orchestra (W39c). "But this
is a symphony with many attractive, memorable
tunes, with movement and some charm. It is
probably not an important work but I will venture
nothing more."

B67. Davis, Peter G. "Miami Opera´s Mega-Bomb." <u>New York</u>
15, no. 25 (June 21, 1982): 60-61.

Review of the premiere of <u>Minutes till Midnight</u>
(W79a). "For all the commendable workmanship, the
music remains gray and neutral, a well-intentioned
but thoroughly pedestrian piece of work."

B68. Dierks, Donald. [untitled review] <u>Musical Times</u> 106
(1965): 204.

Review of a performance of <u>The Crucible</u> at UCLA
(W55m). "Within its conservative frame, Ward´s
musical idiom is lively, unpretentious and easily
grasped. His melodies are the kind which can be
whistled on the way home, and his traditional
harmonies link him with an earlier generation of
American composers."

B69. Dietz, Robert J. "Crucible Review -- Highly
Successful." <u>Iowa City (Iowa) Daily Iowan</u>,
c.August 1, 1962.

Review of a performance of <u>The Crucible</u> at the
State University of Iowa (W55d). "As a whole, the
work is a blend of an almost-Wagnerian orchestral
texture and a singer´s opera."

B70. Downes, Olin. "Brailowsky Wins Audience Acclaim." <u>New
York Times</u>, February 1, 1950.

Review of a performance of <u>Symphony No. 2</u> by the
Philadelphia Orchestra (W31d). "In the sense of
modern orchestral music the Ward work is almost
childish. For genius, task, humor and are, [sic]
the piece is a perfect charmer, fluent and
orthodox."

B71.   Drake, Miles Edward. [untitled review] <u>Opera News</u> 46,
       no. 5 (November 1981): 66.

       Review of a performance of <u>Claudia Legare</u> at Duke
       University (W75b). "... little of the music,
       conservative and romantic in idiom, was memorable."

B72.   Drone, Jeanette. "American Composer Update." <u>Pan
       Pipes</u> 73, no. 2 (Winter 1981): 45; also 75, no. 2
       (Winter 1983): 44-45.

       Lists performances of Ward´s works around the
       world, including some performances not listed in
       this book; also biographical information.

B73.   Dwight, Ogden. "3,000 Hear Premiere of Cantata." <u>Des
       Moines Register</u>, November 21, 1960.

       Review of the premiere of <u>Earth Shall Be Fair</u>
       (W53a). "Ward´s music, too, painted expressive
       accompaniments for the many moods of menace, peril,
       divine anger, human guilt, self-examination, faith
       in the Lord and trust in His goodness and mercy."

B74.   Dye, Bill. "Quincy Little Symphony Presents Modern
       Work before Packed House." <u>Quincy (Ill.) Herald-
       Whig</u>, April 27, 1951.

       Review of the premiere of <u>Sacred Songs for
       Pantheists</u> (W42a). "It is definitely modern in form
       and content. Perhaps it was because of this that
       the song cycle was difficult to grasp and retain
       upon a first hearing.... Perhaps the 34-year-old
       Mr. Ward has composed something that is ahead of
       its times musically, like some of the late works of
       Igor Stravinsky or something by Arnold Schoenberg.
       It is one of those works that you would like to
       discuss with the composer."

B75.   E., R. "´Crucible´ in New Test." <u>New York Herald
       Tribune</u>, c.October 20, 1961.

       Preview of the premiere of <u>The Crucible</u> (W55a).
       "The music is of several varieties. Basically it
       is straight diatonic and there is considerable
       choirlike stuff of a pious hue. But there is also
       strongly romantic music for the love scenes and
       some wildly bizarre episodes for the witches where
       the composer is considering using some taped
       electronic sounds."

B76.   Ehinger, Hans. "Robert Wards ´Hexenjagd´ im Stadt-
       theater." <u>Neue Zeitschrift für Musik</u> 125 (1964):
       74.
       Review of a performance of <u>The Crucible</u> by the
       Stadttheater Bern (W55k). "Das ist bei einem
       Musikdrama wie diesem besonderer Bedeutung, bliebe
       ansonst doch der recht krause Gang der Handlung dem

unvorbereiteten Besucher weitgehend verborgen."

B77. Ellington, Floyd. "Ward´s ´Canticles´ Has Rousing
      Debut." Charlotte (N.C.) Observer, c.May 2, 1976.

      Review of the premiere of the Fifth Symphony
      (W73a). "... an evening of middleweight but
      interesting works."

B78. Engle, Donald. "Gorodnitzky, Ward Feature Concert
      Here." Washington Post, January 26, 1948.

      Review of the premiere Symphony No. 2 (W31a). "...
      the composer has drawn upon the musical forms of
      the past, as the structure in which to incorporate
      his new harmonic and rhythmic idioms."

B79. Epstein, Bob. "Ward´s Opera is New, but Still Old."
      Minneapolis Tribune, April 16, 1978.

      Review of the premiere of Claudia Legare (W75a).
      "Ward´s score, while never quite hitting the level
      of salon music, hardly rises above it, so tired and
      uninspired is his creative spark.... It is very
      tuneful, sometimes lyrical, never dramatic."

B80. Estes, Mary. "From Pulitzer Winner to Pulitzer
      Committee." Charlotte (N.C.) News, April 21, 1976.

      Interview with the composer on the occasion of the
      premiere of the Fifth Symphony (W73a).

B81. Eversman, Alice. "Composition, Artist have Debut in
      National Symphony Concert." Washington Evening
      Star, January 26, 1948.

      Review of the premiere of Symphony No. 2 (W31a).
      "His sense of concretness of form is highly
      developed so that the contour in itself is
      arresting. But he has imagination as well and the
      ability to express it surely and clearly in the
      orchestral range."

B82. Eversman, Alice. "Kindler Opens Sunday Concerts with
      Tschaikowsky, Wagner." Washington Evening Star,
      October 20, 1947.

      Review of a performance of Lamentation by Samuel
      Sorin (W30c). "Ward ... has again written a moving
      piece of sombre intent."

B83. Eversman, Alice. "Ward Scores Success in Conducting
      His Own ´Third Symphony´." Washington Evening Star,
      April 1, 1950.

      Review of the premiere of the Third Symphony
      (W40a). "Mr. Ward stands out for a natural suavity
      in style, for imaginative concept and for a

vitality that never slackens. These were present
in the work given its first performance last
night.... The conciseness in form and the logical
substance in every measure arrests attention."

B84. Evett, Robert. "The New American Operas." New Republic
140, no. 17 (April 27, 1959): 22.

Review of a performance of He Who Gets Slapped by
the New York City Opera Company (W46b). "It was no
doubt Mr. Ward's intention that this opera would be
as tightly unified as possible, with no one element
taking over at the expense of the others. It seems
to me that he has been successful in the highest
degree. Seeing He Who Gets Slapped, I felt that
there was a stature and maturity about it that was
no end flattering to the operatic stage."

B85. Ewen, David. American Composers: A Biographical
Dictionary. London: Robert Hale, 1982.

Excellent critical biography (pp. 699-703), with
bibliography and partial worklist.

B86. Ewen, David. American Composers Today. New York: H.W.
Wilson Co., 1949.

Brief biography (pp. 255-256), mostly in the
composer's own words, with partial worklist.

B87. Ewen, David. The World of Twentieth-Century Music.
Englewood Cliffs: Prentice-Hall, 1968.

Short biography, with discussions of the Symphony
No. 2 (W31) and The Crucible (W55). Of the latter:
"... one of the most significant operas by an
American -- for the nobility, distinction and
dramatic interest of Ward's music and also because
it boasts an extraordinarily effective libretto
derived from a major American play."

B88. Eyer, Ronald. "Ward Shows Theatrical Skill in First
Opera, Pantaloon." Musical America 76, no. 6 (June
1956): 18.

Review of the premiere of Pantaloon (W46a). "[Ward
has] a sure sense of theater, of dramatic surge and
contrast and the all-important matters of
proportion and timing.... Ward also is fecund in
tuneful ideas of grace and profile, and his
word-setting has a naturalness, without monotony,
which stamps him as an uncommonly fine prosodist."

B89. F., A. "Pianist, Composer, Orchestra Praised." Erie
(Pa.) Daily Times, November 20, 1963.

Review of the premiere of Music for a Celebration
(W58a). "Ward has the happy faculty of writing

tuneful music, but in a style which gives it
strength and character."

B90. F., M. "Arthur Millers ´Hexenjagd´ als Oper."
      Schweitzerische Musikzeitung 104 (1964): 51.

      Review of a performance of The Crucible by the
      Stadttheater Bern (W55k). "Damit ist nicht gesagt,
      dass Robert Wards ´Hexenjagd´ schlechtes
      Musiktheater sei, aber es ist nicht mehr Oper im
      Sinne der europäische Entwicklung.... Sie sollte
      nur nicht auf Kosten der künstlerichen
      Selbsändigkeit der Musikgehen, deren Funktion hier
      etwas in der Richtung der Filmmusik gedeutet
      erscheint."

B91. F., W. "Violin and Viola Pieces by Ward and Britten."
      Musical America 72, no. 6 (April 15, 1952): 24.

      Review of the First Sonata for Violin and Piano
      (W40). "... mechanically over-extended, rather
      old-fashioned, and specious in harmonic style."

B92. Farwell, Hal. "´Abélard and Héloise´ Judged a Solid
      Success." Arts Journal 7, no. 6 (March 1982): 31.

      Review of the premiere of Abelard and Heloise
      (W78a). "Ward´s music is intriguing and makes one
      look forward to future hearings.... Nobody went
      home humming the hit tunes, but one could hardly
      escape hearing the heroic overtones that lift his
      song beyond what is merely pretty and seem so
      appropriate to the story ..."

B93. Farwell, Hal. "Impenitent Lovers: Abélard and
      Héloise." Arts Journal 7, no. 5 (February 1982):
      34-35.

      Preview of the premiere of Abelard and Heloise
      (W78a), with an interview with soprano Jacquelyn
      Culpepper.

B94. Farwell, Harold. [untitled review] Opera News 47, no.
      3 (September 1982): 46.

      Review of the premiere of Abelard and Heloise
      (W78a). "The music is lush and lyrical ... Ward´s
      score proved most impressive in lyric moments."

B95. Faust, Carl R. [untitled review] Opera News 40, no. 23
      (June 1976): 44.

      Review of a performance of The Crucible by the
      Florentine Opera (W55ss). "... this production
      failed to deliver so much of the score´s impact
      that by evening´s end an already sparse house was
      decimated by vacated seats ..."

B96.   Fay, John. "Curtin, Ward Win Friends in Mobile." <u>Mobile (Ala.) Register</u>, January 10, 1967.

Review of the premiere of <u>Hymn to the Night</u> (W67a). "It is horizontal composing, a lot of counterpoint between choirs of the orchestra and ... a good exposition of Ward's gift with a melody. The sonorities are of depth and pleasant, the systems of tonality coming back to a firm base."

B97.   Feingold, Michael. "Music Hath Charms." <u>Village Voice</u> 23, no. 5 (January 30, 1978): 67.

Review of a performance of <u>He Who Gets Slapped</u> by the Encompass Theatre (W46e). "The score of <u>Pantaloon</u> is largely academic post-Straussian, an idiom in which many American operas of the period lie buried, as it were, under synthetic <u>schlag</u>."

B98.   Feldman, M.A. [untitled review] <u>Opera News</u> 39, no. 4 (October 1974): 47-48.

Review of a performance of <u>The Crucible</u> by the Des Moines Metropolitan Opera (W55mm). "... a searing conception, with fanaticism and represssed sexuality underscored by symbolic lighting and costuming."

B99.   Feldman, M.A. [untitled review] <u>Opera News</u> 42, no. 22 (June 1978): 34.

Review of the premiere of <u>Claudia Legare</u> (W75a). "He sets the language very well; everything is natural in inflection and singable. There is a line in the libretto, however, that sums up the hazard: 'The old ways are dead ways.'"

B100. Finn, Robert. "'Crucible' at CIM Hard to Understand." <u>Cleveland Plain Dealer</u>, December 8, 1972.

Review of a performance of <u>The Crucible</u> at the Cleveland Institute of Music (W55hh). "Ward's opera is thoroughly traditional in dramatic concept and musical style. Ward makes no attempt to differentiate musically among the many characters, preferring simply to give musical embodiment to the mood and imagery of the text."

B101. Finn, Robert. "'Crucible' Deserves Met's Attentions." <u>Cleveland Plain Dealer</u>, August 20, 1966.

Review of a performance of <u>The Crucible</u> by the Lake George Opera Festival (W55p). "It is a first-rate theater piece, the work of a skilled and imaginative composer who knows how to orchestrate cleanly and how to write for the voice. And one who has the rare and wonderful knack of finding the underlying musical rhythm of English prose."

B102.   First, Wesley. "Robert Ward's Music Pleases Audience."
        Erie Dispatch, December 22, 1948.

        Review of the premiere of Concert Music (W33a). "It
        is a brief, slickly written piece of rather small
        scope but containing considerable harmonic and
        structural interest."

B103.   "Five Operas." Time 67, no. 22 (May 28, 1956): 51.

        Review of the premiere of Pantaloon (W46a).
        "Composer Ward's music resembles Mascagni's, with
        thick textures, sweeping strings and sweet
        harmonies, and thus Pantaloon has the makings of a
        successful theater piece. Unfortunately, the drama
        does not need, or benefit from, the addition of
        music."

B104.   Fleming, Shirley. "Musician of the Month: Robert
        Ward." Musical America 32, no. 5 (May 1982): 4-5.

        Interview with the composer about his operas, on
        the occasion of the premieres of Minutes Till
        Midnight (W78a) and Abelard and Heloise (W79a).

B105.   Fox, Barbara. "Cedar Lane's Opera Works Well."
        Montgomery (County, Md.) Journal, May 25, 1979.

        Review of a performance of He Who Gets Slapped by
        the Cedar Lane Stage (W46f).

B106.   Fraser, Marie. "Appreciative Audiences Needed to
        Support Creativity, Artists Say." Muncie (Indiana)
        Star, June 23, 1963.

        Interview with the composer on the occasion of a
        performance of The Crucible by the Little
        Shoestring Opera Workshop (W55h).

B107.   French, Edward. "Debut Highlights Symphony Program."
        Unidentified newspaper, probably in or near Albany,
        New York, c.May 5, 1980.

        Review of a performances of the Fourth Symphony by
        the Albany Symphony Orchestra in Troy and Albany
        (W52c, W52d). "... a work that deserves to be in
        the repertoire of every major orchestra. In style
        the composer has come up with a feeling of middle
        European romanticism in the slow sections and a
        typically American rhythmic bounce in the fast
        movements, all with a moderately contemporary
        pungency to his harmonic practices."

B108.   Freund, Bob. "Peak Performances Mark Concert Series
        Finale." Fort Lauderdale (Fla.) News, March 29,
        1967.

Review of a performance of <u>Euphony for Orchestra</u> by the Fort Lauderdale Symphony (W43i). "Robert Ward´s Euphony for Orchestra is pastoral in nature, American in atmosphere and richly scored. Ward has a fine touch with lush harmony and the orchestra captured the mood as well as the sonorous qualities handsomely."

B109. Freund, Bob. "´The Crucible´ a Coup." <u>Tribune</u> (unidentified city: Tampa, Florida?), March 21, 1974.

Review of a performance of <u>The Crucible</u> by the Greater Miami International Opera (W551l). "´The Crucible´ may have sounded extremely dissonant when it first debuted, but now it seems hardly that at all, albeit there are some intervals that tax the singers, and some peculiar unresolved endings that curl the hair a bit ... Yet it is great theater, grim, gripping, and at times, musically enthralling, a superb libretto that is aided by a good, if not necessarily great, score."

B110. Fried, Alexander. "Fresh, Powerful ´Crucible´." <u>San Francisco Examiner</u>, June 24, 1965.

Review of a performance of <u>The Crucible</u> by the San Francisco Opera (W55o). "... its whole operatic approach is obvious and practical, rather than deeply novel or searching."

B111. Fuller, Donald. "Russian and American Season, 1945." <u>Modern Music</u> 22 (1945): 254-258.

Review of a number of performances of modern music, including (p. 256) the premiere of <u>Adagio and Allegro</u> (W27a). "... a little too simplified in its attitudes, yet had disarmingly direct speech."

B112. Fuller, Donald. "Winter to Spring, New York, 1942." <u>Modern Music</u> 19 (1942): 173-178.

Review of a number of recent performances of modern music, including the premiere of the <u>First Symphony</u> (W16a). "... disarming in its directness and lack of adornment. It needs more invention and cunning, but the lyrical talent, despite its debt to Ravel, shows real distinction."

B113. G., H. "Wie aus einem Roman." <u>Wiesbadenes Kurier (West Germany)</u>, October 28, 1963.

Preview of a performance of <u>The Crucible</u> by the Hessisches Staattheater (W55j).

B114. Gann, Kyle. [untitled review] <u>Opera News</u> 50, no. 2 (August 1985): 45.

Review of a performance of <u>The Crucible</u> by the
Chicago Opera Theater (W55xx). "Ward's setting is
conservative in its mildly dis[s]onant tonality,
and its melodic flow and stage conventions are
curiously Wagnerian for an American work written in
1961."

B115.   Gelles, George. "Dull Score Deadens 'The Crucible'."
        <u>Washington Star</u>, August 29, 1975.

        Review of a performance of <u>The Crucible</u> by the
        Wolf Trap Company (W55pp). "'The Crucible' is an
        expert piece of work, cunningly wrought and deftly
        fashioned. Ultimately however, it fails to be
        moving. It is admirable but academic, and if every
        note is unarguably in its proper place, the melodic
        thrust is so insipid and the rhythmic impulse so
        banal that it hardly makes much difference."

B116.   George, Earl. [untitled review] <u>Notes</u> 10 (1953):
        496-498.

        Review of <u>Sorrow of Mydath</u> (W9). "... comes
        dangerously close to being a typical concert dirge,
        with its ponderous ostinatos and boiling climax....
        Mr. Ward's taste saves him, if only by a hair's
        breadth."

B117.   Giffin, Glenn. "'Crucible' Is Caldron of Emotion."
        <u>Denver Post</u>, ?c.1975.

        Review of a performance of <u>The Crucible</u> at the
        University of Colorado (W55nn). "Where contemporary
        opera is concerned, the music of Robert Ward
        carries the action and underlying passions
        skillfully, searingly, using the Arthur Miller play
        as his point of departure."

B118.   Goldberg, Albert. "UCLA Opera Group Presents
        'Crucible'." <u>Los Angeles Times</u>, December 5, 1964.

        Review of a performance of <u>The Crucible</u> at UCLA
        (W55m). "On the whole it is a score that commands
        respect for its seriousness and honesty."

B119.   Goodfellow, William S. "Pair of Surprises in St.
        Paul." <u>Chicago Sun-Times</u>, July 11, 1973.

        Review of a performance of <u>The Crucible</u> by the St.
        Paul Opera (W55jj). "... the horrifying
        crosscurrents of the Salem witch trials have called
        forth from the composer a score both ruggedly
        American in its musical fabric -- hymn-tune
        chorales alternating with the rhythmic and harmonic
        patterns of natural speech -- and of appealingly
        melodic directness."

B120.   Goosen, J.F. "5 Top Works Performed at Forum."

<u>Tuscaloosa (Alabama) News</u>, May 3, 1965.

Review of a performance of <u>First Sonata for Violin
and Piano</u> by Julius Hegyi and Charlotte Hegyi
(W40j). "Ward´s sonata is a frankly romantic work,
with a broad lyric line and strenuous climaxes. It
has a good sense of motion, ample instrumental
interest, and clear design. It is a work of
conviction, couched in a personal idiom that
reaches an audience immediately."

B121.   Grondahl, Hilmar. "Cast Receives Opening Night Raves
as Opera Debuts in Colorado Town." <u>Portland Sunday
Oregonian</u>, July 6, 1964.

Review of the premiere of <u>The Lady from Colorado</u>
(W60a). "Ward is a very knowledgeable composer,
and what he has written is done with sincerity and
skill in what he considers the best way to handle
the story material at hand."

B122.   Gunn, Glenn Dillard. "Music: National Gallery Opens
Its New Season Tonight." <u>Washington Times-Herald</u>,
September 12, 1948.

Preview of a performance of the <u>First Symphony</u> by
the National Symphony Orchestra (W16c).

B123.   Gunn, Glenn Dillard. "Ormandy Directs Philadelphians
in Brilliant Concert." <u>Washington Times-Herald</u>,
April 12, 1950.

Review of a peformance of <u>Symphony No. 2</u> by the
Philadelphia Orchestra (W31f). "It is a modern
expression but not cacophonous. Its patterns are
strophic yet not monotonous. They are easily
understood by any listener of moderate concert
experience. Yet the work is original."

B124.   Gunn, Glenn Dillard. "Packed Hall Captivated by
Margaret." <u>Washington Times-Herald</u>, November 28,
1949.

Review of a performance of <u>Adagio and Allegro</u> by
the National Symphony (W27d). "He then brought to a
first hearing here Robert Ward´s <u>Adagio and Allegro</u>
without, it must be confessed, discovering
qualities of music that justified the attention
given it."

B125.   Gunn, Glenn Dillard. "Symphony Reaches New High with
´Francesca da Rimini." <u>Washington Times-Herald</u>,
October 20, 1947.

Review of a performance of <u>Lamentation</u> by Samuel
Sorin (W30c). "... the ear is refreshed with new
sounds of unmistakable eloquence."

B126. Gunn, Glenn Dillard. "Two Gallery Concerts Mix
       Ancient and Modern Music." <u>Washington Times-Herald</u>,
       October 10, 1949.

       Review of a performance of <u>Night Music</u> by the
       National Gallery Orchestra (W37b). "Ward´s ´Night
       Music,´ though little more than a sympathetic
       tribute to Gershwin is developed with imagination."

B127. H., C. "Sorkin Plays Violin in 3d Program Here." <u>New
       York Times</u>, September 29, 1950.

       Review of a performance of <u>First Sonata for Violin
       and Piano</u> by Herbert Sorkin and Brooks Smith
       (W40b). "Mr. Ward´s Sonata is an amiable work that
       draws easily on French thematic periodicity and the
       energetic dissonances of Bartók. It suffers from
       inability to sustain its several stabs at
       rhythmical drive, always falling back into a
       pastoral kind of melody..."

B128. H., J. "Composer Pleased With New ´Music´." <u>Erie (Pa.)
       Daily Times</u>, November 20, 1963.

       Interview with the composer on the occasion of the
       premiere of <u>Music for a Celebration</u> (W58a).

B129. Haley, Pope. "´Crucible´ Deserves Its Bicentennial
       Designation." <u>Jacksonville (Fla.) Times-Union and
       Journal</u>, February 1, 1976.

       Review of a performance of <u>The Crucible</u> by the
       Jacksonville Opera Repertory Group (W55rr). "There
       are few if any other extant works, either in
       dramatic or operatic form, so solidly founded in
       American history and folklore, or more thoroughly
       American in concept, creation and production than
       this highly dramatic work."

B130. Hamburger, Philip. "Gingery Snare." <u>New Yorker</u> 25,
       no. 51 (February 11, 1950): 74-75.

       Review of the premiere of <u>Jonathon and the Gingery
       Snare</u> (W38a). "The Young People, I should say, were
       enthralled by ´Jonathon,´ and found it exactly to
       their taste. Even the extremely active [paper-
       airplane] flying school in the upper regions
       cancelled all their flights during this number. I
       hope Mr. Ward´s jolly little piece will turn up
       soon on records, so that it will be enjoyed by a
       larger audience."

B131. Harvey, John H. "´Claudia´ Updates Ibsen with
       Clarity." <u>St. Paul Sunday Pioneer Press</u>, April 16,
       1978.

       Review of the premiere of <u>Claudia Legare</u> (W75a).
       "In his conservative style, Ward has written vocal

lines which are charged dramatically and always are eminently singable. The orchestral writing skillfully and effectively creates atmosphere, heightens the dramatic moments and also is unobtrusively supportive when the focus is on the vocal lines."

B132.   Harvey, John H.   "´Crucible´ Done with Distinction." St. Paul Pioneer Press, May 2, 1969.

Review of a performance of The Crucible by the St. Paul Opera Association (W55y). "[The play] was invested with music which, on the one hand, is both eminently singable and expressive of text, and on the other maintains and heightens the dramatic flow."

B133.   Harvey, John H.   "´The Crucible´ Performance Brilliant and Persuasive." St. Paul Dispatch, June 21, 1973.

Review of a performance of The Crucible by the St. Paul Opera (W55jj). "I happen to consider ´The Crucible´ a solid piece of work and believe that on balance more in dimensions are added by the music than are lost in the transference ... to the operatic medium."

B134.   H[arvey] J[ohn H.] "Encompass Theatre: ´Pantaloon, He Who Gets Slapped." High Fidelity 28, no. 5 (May 1978): MA26.

Review of a performance of He Who Gets Slapped by the Encompass Theatre (W46e). "The style is more conservative, and almost ostentatious in its variety."

B135.   Harvey, John H. "Minnesota Opera Company: Robert Ward´s ´Claudia Legare´." High Fidelity 28, no. 8 (August 1978): MA17-18.

Review of the premiere of Claudia Legare (W75a). "Within the dramatic flow of Ibsen´s play Stambler and Ward have found ample opportunities for numerous set-pieces which work well both dramatically and musically."

B136.   Harvey, John H. "Opera Association´s ´Crucible´ Called Refreshing Experience." St. Paul Dispatch, May 2, 1969.

Review of a performance of The Crucible by the St. Paul Opera Association (W55y). "[Ward] is an old-fashioned composer in the sense that he recognizes a difference between orchestral instruments and singers and believes the latter should be ... given singable music which directly expresses the text and moves in recognizably melodic patterns."

B137.   Harvey, John H.   "Opera Has Ibsen Drama Set in
        Postbellum South." St. Paul Pioneer Press, April 9,
        1978.

        Interview with the composer on the occasion of the
        premiere of Claudia Legare (W75a).

B138.   Haskins, John.   "Music in Mid-America." Kansas City
        Times, September 18, 1968.

        Review of a performance of The Crucible by the
        Kansas City Lyric Theater (W55x). "... a production
        of Robert Ward's melodramatic 'The Crucible' that
        was nicely paced, superbly staged, and earnestly
        played and sung."

B139.   Haskins, John.   "'Witchcraft' in Opera Tonight."
        Kansas City Times, September 17, 1968.

        Preview of a performance of The Crucible by the
        Kansas City Lyric Theater (W55x), with an interview
        with the composer.

B140.   Hewes, Henry.   "New Stars Icumen In." Saturday Review
        39, no. 23 (June 9, 1956): 27.

        Review of the premiere of Pantaloon (W46a). "While
        'Pantaloon' contains a great deal of competent and
        intelligent work, it emerges as a
        not-exciting-enough attempt to adapt a great
        European play to the American musical stage."

B141.   Hirschberg, Nell.   "Superb Music, Singing Mark
        Premiere of Opera at Duke." Raleigh (N.C.) News
        and Observer, February 25, 1982.

        Review of a performance of Abelard and Heloise by
        the North Carolina Opera in Durham (W78c). "He has
        set a libretto by Jan Hartman to music
        appropriately lyrical and dramatic as demanded by
        'the legend and history of France's most famous
        lovers.'"

B142.   Holbert, Allan.   "Miller's 'The Crucible' Presented by
        St. Paul Opera Association." Minneapolis Tribune,
        May 2, 1969.

        Review of a performance of The Crucible by the St.
        Paul Opera Association (W55y). "The opera is
        written in traditional opera form, but the score is
        of a fairly contemporary nature and it serves the
        plot well."

B143.   Holl.   "American Opera Cycle." Variety, April 15,
        1959.

        Review of a performance of He Who Gets Slapped by

the New York City Opera Company (W46b). "... it has
the earmarks of becoming a popular offering
although the more demanding opera buffs may not
find it sufficiently advanced."

B144. Hoover, Joanne Sheehy. "Cedar Lane´s ´He Who Gets
Slapped´ First-Rate." <u>Washington Post</u>, May 17,
1979.

Review of a performance of <u>He Who Gets Slapped</u> by
the Cedar Lane Stage (W46f). "Those fearful of
dissonant contemporary works can rest easy because
Ward sits squarely in the Romantic tradition, which
means that he believes in melodies. ´He Who Gets
Slapped´ is filled with flowing lines that are a
joy for singers and audiences alike."

B145. Horton, Charles. "Music Fatally Flaws Duke Opera
Offering." <u>Chapel Hill (N.C.) Newspaper</u>, July 30,
1981.

Review of a performance of <u>Claudia Legare</u> in Durham
(W75b). "... Ward has remained loyal to a tonal and
post-romantic style of writing throughout several
decades of battering from avant garde and atonal
devotees. The strong influence of Howard Hanson
and the Eastman School are most evident, but he
seems to have chosen the best elements of this
influence and combined them with an individualistic
and imaginative style of his own."

B146. Hruby, Frank. "A Dulled Edge." <u>Musical America</u> 82,
no. 11 (December 1962): 15.

Review of a performance of <u>Euphony for Orchestra</u> by
the Cleveland Orchestra (W43f). "It has a friendly
warmth, indigenous rhythms, and many of the long,
lyrical lines for which Ward has become famous."

B147. Hruby, Frank. "An Ibsen Girl Reborn in Dixie."
<u>Cleveland Press</u>, April 15, 1978.

Review of the premiere of <u>Claudia Legare</u> (W75a).
"His style is unabashedly romantic and he resists
all urges to write ´modern´ music. ´Claudia
Legare´ is meant to sing, to fee[l], to animate its
characters with hot blood, not captive stultified
romance."

B148. Hruby, Frank. "Karamu Opera Cast Fine in ´He Who Gets
Slapped´." <u>Cleveland Press</u>, June 1, 1961.

Review of a performance of <u>He Who Gets Slapped</u> by
the Karamu Theatre (W46c). "Ward´s music does not
particularly belong to any school. He sets the
words to music so that they are, first of all
understandable. Then he makes sure that they
follow a musical path that is attractive and

appropriate."

B149.   Hruby, Frank. "Orchestra Features Cleveland
        Composer." Cleveland Press, October 19, 1962.

        Review of a performance of Euphony for Orchestra by
        the Cleveland Orchestra (W43f). "It has a friendly
        warmth, a modicum of indigenous rhythms, and many
        long, lyrical lines for which Ward has become
        well-known.... The piece avoids the trickiness
        that many contemporary composers employ and thus is
        a direct, pleasant expression of conservative
        ideas."

B150.   Hruby, Frank. "Strong Music Institute Cast Gives
        'Crucible' Authority." Cleveland Press, December 7,
        1972.

        Review of a performance of The Crucible at the
        Cleveland Institute of Music (W55hh). "Ward's opera
        provides much for everyone the sing and act. It
        resorts to no contemporary tricks or gimmicks and
        relies entirely on tradition-oriented structures to
        provide the emotion and drama."

B151. Huber, Harold. [untitled review.] Opera 27 (1976): 721.

        Review of a performance of The Crucible by the
        Florentine Opera (W55ss). "... one could feel the
        involvement of the unusually hushed audience
        throughout the performance."

B152.   Huff, Serge. "'Hymn and Celebration' Well Received by
        Audience." Phoenix (Ariz.) Gazette, March 28, 1962.

        Review of the premiere of Hymn and Celebration
        (W56a). "It appears that Ward has fallen into the
        trap that so many other American composers have --
        that of feeling they must use something strictly
        American with which to characterize their music --
        invariably the jazz idiom is selected as the device
        to satisfy this requirement."

B153.   Hughes, Allen. "A Schirmer Work Given at Festival."
        New York Times, June 25, 1968.

        Review of the premiere of the Concerto for Piano
        and Orchestra (W69a). "The Ward Concerto ... is
        apparently a recent work, but it would pass for a
        holdover from the 1940's. It begins with triads in
        the manner of the Copland of two decades ago and
        never wanders appreciably or interestingly among
        the harmonic possibilities available today."

B154.   Humphreys, Henry S. "Francescatti Plays Paganini with
        Symphony." Cincinnati Times-Star, April 3, 1954.

        Review of a performance of the Third Symphony by

the Cincinnati Symphony Orchestra (W39c) "In short,
Ward´s ´Symphony No. 3´ would be most rewarding for
further hearing and study. Certainly it stands
high above numberless other contemporary works of
its scope because of its sincerity and
craftsmanship."

B155.   J[acobs], A[rthur]. [untitled review] <u>Opera</u> 14
(1963): 760-761.

Review of the recording of <u>The Crucible</u> (D5). "...
the gramophone, as usual, ´exposes´ the music, and
I am not entirely convinced by it."

B156.   Jacobson, Robert. [untitled review] <u>Opera News</u> 47,
no. 3 (September 1982): 48.

Review of the premiere of <u>Minutes till Midnight</u>
(W79a). "Ward´s music lent little vitality,
veering as it did between Strauss, Hindemith,
Rogers and Bernstein, among others."

B157.   Jaffe, Jody. "Debut of ´Abelard and Heloise´ Makes
Charlotte a Premiere City." <u>Charlotte (N.C.)
Observer</u>, Febuary 20, 1982.

News story on events surrounding the premiere of
<u>Abelard and Heloise</u> (W78a).

B158.   "Japan Company to Perform Opera." <u>Durham (N.C.)
Morning Herald</u>, May 5, 1983.

News story on a performance of <u>The Crucible</u> by the
Kansai Nikikai Opera Company (W55vv).

B159.   Johnson, Harriet. "City Opera Revives ´The
Crucible´." <u>New York Post</u>, March 9, 1968.

Review of a performance of <u>The Crucible</u> by the New
York City Opera (W55u). "As a drama in music, ...
the work undoubtedly sustains Miller´s belief in
it. Repetitions reinforce rather then [sic] negate
its value."

B160.   Johnson, Harriet. "City Opera Sings First
´Crucible´." <u>New York Post</u>, October 27, 1961.

Review of the premiere of <u>The Crucible</u> (W55o). "...
Ward and Stambler have produced in ´The Crucible´ an
absorbing music drama. The play builds tension in
the manner of a thriller and so does the opera. It
is rhythmically jagged enough to slash as it moves,
yet it is singable."

B161.   Johnson, Harriet. "Opera Gives Gloomy Andreyev
Light." <u>New York Post</u>, April 13, 1959.

Review of a performance of <u>He Who Gets Slapped</u> by

the New York City Opera Company (W46b). "In
general, Ward writes ´numbers´ instead of
galvanizing his music into dramatic synthesis. His
style misses definitive characterization or
personality."

B162. Johnson, Harriet. "Ward Symphony; Manicelli Debut."
       New York Post, March 18, 1959.

       Review of a performance of the Fourth Symphony by
       the National Orchestral Association (W52b). "Ward´s
       composition demonstrates an enviable skill in
       symphonic construction, combined with a spontaneous
       flow and interchange of melodic ideas..... [The
       tunes are] so obvious as to be popular in vein,
       with their corresponding development in the same
       mold."

B163. Johnson, Wayne. "Afterthoughts on ´Crucible´." Times
       (unidentified city), February 11, 1968.

       Interview with the composer after the Seattle Opera
       production of The Crucible (W55t).

B164. Johnson, Wayne. "´Crucible´ Is Disappointing." Times
       (unidentified city), January 31, 1968.

       Review of a performance of The Crucible by the
       Seattle Opera (W55t). "In short, the musical
       aspects of the music-drama form that is opera were
       well realized last night, but the dramatic factors
       were not effectively created. And because the
       drama didn´t come to life, the music, although
       generally good, seemed rather unconnected to any
       present stage reality."

B165. Jones, Abe D., Jr. [untitled review] Greensboro (N.C.)
       News and Record, July 20, 1986.

       Review of the premiere of Festival Triptych (W85a).
       "... has touches of a swing-era ballad in its
       second section and in its concluding ´Vivo´ offers
       a playful pastiche of sounds representing the
       highlights of an evening concert."

B166. Joslyn, Jay. "Symphony Opens with Gala Zest."
       Milwaukee Sentinel, c.October 4, 1966.

       Review of the premiere of Festive Ode (W65a). "Its
       modernity is highlighted by a pulsing statement of
       optimism and vigor instead of the lugubrious and
       dissonant stutter which usually passes for the
       music of our time."

B167. Kastendieck, Miles. "American Work Scores in Bow."
       New York Journal-American, April 13, 1959.

       Review of a performance of He Who Gets Slapped by

the New York City Opera Company (W46b). "Ward has
written with a professional touch. His arias and
duets are clearly defined. They sound more skilled
than his choruses. With him the voice comes first,
for some of the orchestra part sounds more
background than integral."

B168. Kastendieck, Miles. "Bravo, ´Crucible´." New York
       Journal-American, November 12, 1961.

       Review of the premiere of The Crucible (W55a).
       "Ward may show influences of European origin, but
       his music reflects intelligent digestion and
       individual assertion. Since he met the challenge
       of the final scene, the opera emerges as one of the
       most distinctive of our native products. Some may
       nominate it the finest to date."

B169. Kastendieck, Miles. "Forge Triumph in ´Crucible´."
       New York Journal-American, October 27, 1961.

       Review of the premiere of The Crucible (W55a).
       "Just as the story has its consonance and
       dissonance, so Ward´s music matches this in sound.
       This is traditional operatic writing shaped within
       contemporary idiom. Operagoers must again adjust
       to further proof that the lyric theatre is a play
       sung. Miller can be pleased that the music
       enhances the drama, while Ward can bow for
       accomplishing what some might consider impossible.
       ´The Crucible´ is notable achievement in the annals
       of native opera."

B170. Kastendieck, Miles. "National Group´s 3d Program."
       New York Journal-American, March 18, 1959.

       Review of a performance of the Fourth Symphony by
       the National Orchestral Association (W52b). "Ward´s
       symphony is well made, quite respectable, indeed
       surprisingly conservative.... The orchestration is
       good, the skill is there; only individuality is
       lacking. Did he make some compromise in style?"

B171. Kastendieck, Miles. "´3 Oranges´ Enjoyable Opera."
       New York Journal-American, September 29, 1950.

       Review of a performance of First Sonata for Violin
       and Piano by Herbert Sorkin and Brooks Smith
       (W40b.) "... a pleasant enough work, technically
       facile and expressively fluent."

B172. Kendall, Raymond. See also B176 (Kerr, Russell).

B173. Kendall, Raymond. [untitled review] Musical Courier
       158, no. 3 (September 1958): 16.

       Review of the premiere of Symphony No. 4 (W52a).
       "Ward is a thorough craftsman and an ingenuous

[sic] orchestrator. Add to these the fact that he loves a good tune and you might almost predict the kind of satisfying music he turns out."

B174.   Kenyon, Nicholas. "Fine Feeling for Sudden Shock." The (London) Times, June 6, 1984.

Review of a performance of The Crucible by the Abbey Opera (W55ww). "Ward draws his musical ideas from anywhere in sight -- the dissonance is never stronger than in Barber or mild Copland -- and he welds them together with a fine feeling for sudden shock and intense rhapsody."

B175.   Kerner, Leighton. "Bomb over Miami." Village Voice 27, no. 26 (June 29, 1982): 92.

Review of the premiere of Minutes till Midnight (W79a). "Ward's music is not quite so bad [as the libretto]; at least, it's professionally crafted and moves fluently along on puffs of singable tunes. But the score is as blandly 'safe' as the same composer's 20-year-old opera, The Crucible."

B176.   K[err], R[ussell] [or possibly Raymond Kendall]. "He Who Gets Slapped, by Robert Ward." Musical Courier 159, no. 6 (May 1959): 14.

Review of a performance of He Who Gets Slapped by the New York City Opera (W46b). "The music is smoothly and exotically orchestrated, and succeeds best when it allows the solo voices to emerge clearly."

B177.   Kerr, Russell. "A Pulitzer and Two Tchaikowskys." Music Magazine/Musical Courier 164, no. 6 (July 1962): 6-7.

Interview with the composer after his Pulitzer Prize.

B178.   Kimball, George H. "Philharmonic Concert Pleases." Rochester (N.Y.) Times-Union, January 31, 1958.

Review of a performance of the Third Symphony by the Rochester Philharmonic Orchestra (W39e). "Ward's symphony, which is harmonicaly only mildly unconventional, reveals the composer as a gifted melodist and a thorough craftsman of form and orchestration. The work is appealingly melodic, especially in the slow middle movement, and the orchestral resonances throughout are gratifying."

B179.   "Kindler Rehearses Symphony for Opening Concert Oct. 14." Washington Evening Star, October 5, 1948.

Preview of the scheduled premiere (which never took place) of the Serenade for Strings (W34), with an interview with the composer.

B180. Klein, Mitchell. "Concert is Up with Trends."
       Winston-Salem (N.C.) Journal, February 5, 1969.

       Review of a performance of Concerto for Piano and
       Orchestra by Marjorie Mitchell and the
       Winston-Salem Symphony (W69b). "The concerto is
       contemporary, chiefly because of its immersion in
       modern American musical culture, recalling jazz and
       folk music."

B181. Kolodin, Irving. "Aria without an Opera; Opera
       without an Aria." Saturday Review 51, no. 12
       (March 23, 1968): 53-54.

       Review of a performance of The Crucible by the New
       York City Opera (W55u). "... the rehearing attested
       that in his investigation of time, temper, and
       locale, Ward achieved a result that can be heard
       not once or twice but repeatedly with interest and
       enjoyment."

B182. K[olodin], I[rving]. "Barzin Ends Season." New York
       Sun, May 21, 1946.

       Review of a performance of Jubilation and Adagio
       and Allegro by the National Orchestral Association
       (W27b, W28a). "Both show a firm grasp of the
       fundamentals of orchestral writing, especially the
       large-scale orchestra of Wagner and Strauss, with
       numerous brass."

B183. Kolodin, Irving. "Floyd of 'Wuthering Heights' --
       Ward, Foss." Saturday Review 42, no. 17 (April 25,
       1959): 24.

       Review of a performance of He Who Gets Slapped by
       the New York City Opera Company (W46b). "... the
       elements [of the original story] and their appeal
       seem, at the end, more or less where they had been
       in the beginning -- inherent in the subject and
       waiting to be treated, but never quite brought into
       focus by the score."

B184. Kolodin, Irving. "A Second View of Ward's 'Crucible'."
       Saturday Review 45, no. 51 (December 29, 1962): 55.

       Review of the recording of The Crucible (D5).
       "What emerges from the sound alone is the
       overpowering conviction of Ward in the importance
       of his subject ... and his success in converting
       that conviction into musical meaning."

B185. Kolodin, Irving. "Ward on Miller's 'Crucible' --
       Ebert's 'Cosi' -- Alva." Saturday Review 44, no. 45
       (November 11, 1961): 59.

Review of the premiere of The Crucible (W55a). "The
talents that went into his treatment of Andreyev's
'He Who Gets Slapped' ... are here under more
constant discipline, with rising stride of purpose
as the evening progresses."

B186.   "Koreans to Hear Duke Prof's Opera." Durham (N.C.)
Morning Herald, July 16, 1985.

News story on a performance of The Crucible in
Seoul (W55yy).

B187.   Kozinn, Allan. "American Eclectic." Opera News 46,
no. 20 (June 1982): 24-28, 43.

Interview with the composer about his operas, on
the occasion of the premiere of Minutes Till
Midnight (W79a).

B188.   Kratzenstein, Marilou, and Bruce Gustafson. "The
Minneapolis-St. Paul AGO Convention." Diapason 71,
no. 8 (August 1980): 4-5.

Review of the premiere of Celebrations of God in
Nature (W76a). "... this is a broadly-sketched,
traditionally oriented work in three movements."

B189.   Kriegsman, Alan. "Ginastera Bows to Young Composers."
Washington Post, June 24, 1968.

Review of the premiere of the Concerto for Piano
and Orchestra (W69a). "Here the recipe calls for
dabs of Gershwin, Grieg, Rachmaninoff and Grofe,
ever so skillfully blended."

B190.   Kriegsman, Alan. "'Lucky' Operatic Success."
Washington Post, August 29, 1975 (also in August
30).

Interview with the composer on the occasion of a
performance of The Crucible by the Wolf Trap
Company (W55pp).

B191.   Kriegsman, Alan M. "Northern Va. Version of
'Crucible' Is Good Entertainment." Washington
Post, April 27, 1968.

Review of a performance of The Crucible by the
Opera Theatre of Northern Virginia (W55w). "Though
there are no tunes one could call memorable, the
music is more than sufficiently melodious, and the
scoring achieves its effects with skill. On the
whole, however, 'effects' are all that is there.
Not once does the music rise to the dramatic
electricity of Miller's play. The score's
saccharine veneer, in fact, rules out all the
tragic implications of 'The Crucible' and reduces
it to rather crass melodrama."

B192. Kriegsman, Alan. "A Sturdy, Stirring, Admirable
      ´Crucible´." <u>Washington Post</u>, August 29, 1975 (also
      in August 30).

      Review of a performance of <u>The Crucible</u> by the Wolf
      Trap Company (W55pp). "The opera itself is a good,
      stageworthy piece of work which rises in its best
      moments to passages of genuine eloquence and
      passion. Like the play on which it is based, the
      music is dramatically convincing but never as deep
      as its ambitions would make it, and Ward´s honest,
      solid, accessible workmanship is a bit on the bland
      side."

B193. Kyle, Marguerite Kelly. "AmerAllegro." <u>Pan Pipes</u>:
          47, no. 2 (January 1955): 70.
          50, no. 2 (January 1958): 70-76.
          51, no. 2 (January 1959): 87-88.
          52, no. 2 (January 1960): 75.
          53, no. 2 (January 1961): 79.
          54, no. 2 (January 1962): 76.
          55, no. 2 (January 1963): 75.
          56, no. 2 (January 1964): 84-85.
          57, no. 2 (January 1965): 83.
          58, no. 2 (January 1966): 90.
          59, no. 2 (January 1967): 100.

      Lists performances of Ward´s works around the
      world, including some performances not listed in
      this book; also biographical information.

B194. Lambert, John W. "Give Peace a Chance." <u>Raleigh
      (N.C.) Spectator</u>, June 4-10, 1987.

      Review of the premiere of <u>Dialogue on the Tides of
      Time</u> (W86a). "As conducted by the composer, this
      was unquestionably the emotional highlight of the
      evening and ... made a powerful impression. It
      will be good to hear it again in a different venue,
      the better to assess its purely musical qualities."

B195. Lambert, John W. "Ward to the Wise." <u>Raleigh (N.C.)
      Spectator</u>, February 6, 1986.

      Review of the premiere of the <u>Raleigh Divertimento</u>
      (W84a) and a performance of <u>The Crucible</u> at Duke
      University (W55zz). "[The <u>Raleigh Divertimento</u>] is
      an important original composition which should have
      great success and many performances around the
      world... [<u>The Crucible</u>] was a gripping theatrical
      experience that left a good many members of the
      audience stunned and emotionally drained. Somehow,
      one suspects that this is precisely what Messrs.
      Miller, Stambler and Ward had in mind all along."

B196. Lang, Paul Henry. "Opera First Night: ´The
      Crucible´." <u>New York Herald Tribune</u>, October 27,

1961.

Review of the premiere of <u>The Crucible</u> (W55a).
"Robert Ward's music gallantly and honestly strives
to wring all the drama it can out of the libretto,
so much so that the effect is often more theatrical
than in the deepest sense dramatic, and is more a
matter of idiom than meaning. We observe the work
of a good operatic composer who holds our interest
because something is always happening, and keeps us
on the alert because that something is always
changing, and by the seriousness of action and
thought preserves the edge of emotions always
sharp."

B197.   L[ang], P[aul] H[enry]. [untitled review]   <u>Musical</u>
        <u>Quarterly</u> 48 (1962): 99-104.

        Review of a number of recent performances,
        including (pp. 102-104) the premiere of <u>The</u>
        <u>Crucible</u> (W55a). Adapted from B196 above,
        including the quotation.

B198.   Lang, Phyllis. "Saxophone Concerto Premieres in
        Charlotte." <u>Arts Journal</u> 9, no. 5 (February 1984):
        37.

        Preview of the premiere of the <u>Concerto for</u>
        <u>Saxophone</u> (W81a).

B199.   Larsen, Robert L. "A Study and Comparison of Samuel
        Barber's <u>Vanessa</u>, Robert Ward's <u>The Crucible</u>, and
        Gunther Schuller's <u>The Visitation</u>." D.M. disserta-
        tion, Indiana University, 1971.

        Analysis and discussion of three contemporary
        American operas, including <u>The Crucible (W55)</u>.

B200.   L[evinger], H[enry] W. [untitled review] <u>Musical</u>
        <u>Courier</u> 154, no. 1 (July 1956): 9-10.

        Review of the premiere of <u>Pantaloon</u> (W46a). "It is
        the work of a composer with a vivid sense for stage
        effects, though sometimes the music ... is
        epigonal, and the orchestration ... and melodic
        structure musical comedy-ish.... Mr. Ward has
        written a musical melodrama of genuine theatrical
        excitement."

B201.   Lewis, Beverly. "Composer, Librettist Note Special
        Efforts for Effect." <u>Iowa City (Iowa) Daily Iowan</u>,
        c.August 1, 1962.

        Interview with Ward and Bernard Stambler on the
        occasion of a performance of <u>The Crucible</u> at the
        State University of Iowa (W55d).

B202.   Lippincott, Joe, and Joe Kirkish. "Pulitzer Prize

Winning Opera in Iowa City -- 'The Crucible.'."
Iowa City (Iowa) Daily Iowan, August 1, 1962.

Picture story on a performance of The Crucible at
the State University of Iowa (W55d).

B203.   Little, Barbara. "Audience Warmly Receives Pulitzer
Prize Composer." *Lancaster (Pa.) Intelligencer
Journal*, April 30, 1979.

Review of a performance of the Prairie Overture and
the second movement of the Divertimento for
Orchestra by the Lancaster Symphony Orchestra
(W51j, W54e), with an interview of the composer.
"Ward's compositions were colorfully orchestrated
and had many melodic passages. He made good use of
the various instruments, including the harp. He
was loud and brassy at times and at others, subdued
and melodious."

B204.   Lucas, Urith. "Stage, Film Music Aids New Sounds."
Albuquerque (N. M.) Tribune, October 22, 1964.

Preview of a performance of Euphony for Orchestra
by the Albuquerque Civic Symphony (W43h), with an
interview with the composer. "The Ward composition
on tonight's concert is melodic, marked by
interesting contrast and is a score that keeps
musicians on the alert."

B205.   Margrave, Wendell. "Symphony by Orrego-Salas Tops
Concert at Pavilion." Unidentified newspaper, June
24, 1968.

Review of the premiere of the Concerto for Piano
and Orchestra (W69a). "The work is competently
written, but is something of a collector's item,
with rather too transparent reference to some
well-known piano music by Gershwin."

B206.   Martin, Linton. "Brailowsky Is Soloist at Academy."
Philadelphia Inquirer, January 28, 1950.

Review of a performance of Symphony No. 2 by the
Philadelphia Orchestra (W31d). "Robert Ward's
Second Symphony, the contemporary novelty [of the
program], is a credit to its 32-year-old composer,
and can easily hold its own amid much modern
music."

B207.   Maschal, Richard. "A Bicentennial Baby." *Charlotte
(N.C.) Observer*, April 25, 1976.

Interview with the composer on the occasion of the
premiere of the Fifth Symphony (W73a).

B208.   Maschal, Richard. "Oratorio Singers Triumph in
'Canticles of America'." *Charlotte (N.C.) Observer*,

May 2, 1976.

Review of the premiere of the <u>Fifth Symphony</u>
(W73a). "The work is as American as apple pie, full
of the spirit of our sweet country -- its vastness,
humor, strength, good nature, and, yes, its naivete
and its long painful struggle to fulfill its
ideals."

B209. Mattson, Melanie. "Reprise: The Crucible." <u>Minnesota</u>
       <u>Daily</u>, c.June 21, 1973.

       Review of a performance of <u>The Crucible</u> by the St.
       Paul Opera (W55jj). "Robert Ward's music is
       expressive, if mostly unobtrusive. The recitatives
       and arias have nearly the flow of normal speech
       patterns. He occasionally inserts some noteworthy
       musical effects ... which heighten the musicality
       of the opera and give it a definitely American
       flavor."

B210. Maxwell, Margaret. "The Changing Settlement School."
       <u>Music Journal</u> 11, no. 3 (March 1953): 13, 46.

       Interview with Ward concerning his work at the
       Third Street Music School.

B211. McAdams, Kathy. "'Claudia LeGare' [sic]: Weak Script,
       but Score, Cast Compensate." <u>Durham (N.C.) Morning</u>
       <u>Herald</u>, July 30, 1981.

       Review of a performance of <u>Claudia Legare</u> in Durham
       (W75b). "... an accomplished performance of the
       opera's melodic score"

B212. McEwen, Charles. "Clowns: 'Deadly Serious'."
       <u>Winston-Salem (N.C.) Twin City Sentinel</u>, April 9,
       1973.

       Preview of a performance of <u>He Who Gets Slapped</u> at
       the North Carolina School of the Arts (W46d), with
       an interview with Lesley Hunt and David Marshall,
       who play Tilly and Polly.

B213. McPhail, Claire. "'Abelard and Heloise' Exciting
       World Premiere." <u>Charleston (S.C.) News & Courier</u>
       <u>and Evening Post</u>, February 28, 1982.

       Review of the premiere of <u>Abelard and Heloise</u>
       (W78a). "Ward's opera may earn him another
       Pulitzer, for it has much going for it even though
       it doesn't send you away humming arias or themes.
       It is romantic, dramatic, poignant and completely
       theatrical."

B214. McPhail, Claire. "Symphony Concert Unfamiliar Dose."
       <u>Charleston (S.C.) News and Courier</u>, March 19, 1972.

Review of a performance of <u>Euphony for Orchestra</u> by
the Charleston Symphony Orchestra (W43m). "... it
was for these ears a work of unusual charm. At
times it sounded almost a bit like it might be
built on a folk tune. The changes were interesting
and the climaxes existing [sic]."

B215. McPhee, Colin. "Scores and Records." <u>Modern Music</u> 20
(1943): 204-205.

Review of a number of new works, including the
<u>First Symphony</u> (W16). "... a bright and promising
work by a young composer fairly new on the scene.
The movements are short and to the point; the
orchestration is conventional but clear and direct.
The style is not yet very personal, but one likes
the work for its animation and the zest with which
it seems to have been written."

B216. Melrose, Frances. "´The Lady from Colorado´ Belle of
Central City Opera." <u>Denver Rocky Mountain News</u>,
July 4, 1964.

Review of the premiere of <u>The Lady from Colorado</u>
(W60a). "... modern but, at the same time,
tuneful. At least four arias are decide[d]ly
catchy tunes that should be popular recordings."

B217. M[erkling], F[rank]. [untitled review] <u>Opera News</u> 31,
no. 3 (October 15, 1966): 23.

Review of a performance of <u>The Crucible</u> by the Lake
George Opera Festival (W55p). "Robert Ward´s opera
continues to impress as a straightforward,   ˅
rhythmically incisive setting of a fine play..."

B218. M[erkling], F[rank]. "City Center -- II." <u>Opera News</u>
26, no. 4 (December 9, 1961): 33.

Review of the premiere of <u>The Crucible</u> (W55a).
"... the score adds ... a non-topical sense of the
development of greatness in the human spirit."

B219. M[erkling], F[rank]. "Gotham Demigods." <u>Opera News</u>
21, no. 3 (November 19, 1956): 19.

Review of the premiere of <u>Pantaloon</u> (W46a). "At
times unabashedly reminiscent, especially of
Puccini, his score impressed by its affirmative
lyricism and simple sense of theatre."

B220. Miller, Margo. "´The Crucible´: Moving Music, Strong
Story." <u>Boston Herald</u>, February 15, 1963.

Review of a performance of <u>The Crucible</u> at the New
England Conservatory (W55f). "The tension of
Ward´s musical setting reminds me a little of
portions of <u>Porgy and Bess</u>. It worked for Gershwin

and it certainly works for Ward and for the
performers."

B221. Miller, Robert. "School Gives Concert." Durham (N.C.)
Morning Herald, November 16, 1974.

Review of a performance of Symphony No. 2 by the
North Carolina School of the Arts Orchestra (W31m).
" ... typifies the qualities of American music of a
generation later -- brash harmonies which still
retain their freshness, unabashedly melodic slow
movements and syncopated r[h]ythmic vitality."

B222. Milstein, Frederic. "Operatic Version of Miller Play
Offered." Los Angeles Times, April 17, 1970.

Review of a performance of The Crucible at
California State University at Long Beach (W55z).
"Amalgamated into 'The Crucible' at Cal State Long
Beach Wednesday night were the elements of college
opera at its best: marvelously precise musical
preparation, youthful verve, and enunciators who
almost spelled out every word of their English
text."

B223. Mitchell, Hobart. [untitled review] Notes 9 (1952):
332-333.

Review of (1) Rain Has Fallen All the Day (W13),
(2) As I Watched the Ploughman Ploughing (W10), and
(3) Vanished (W17).

(1) "Ward's writing is thoroughly satisfactory, and
his melody has grace and simplicity. It is a
delightful song." (2) "... he has written a
setting ... which is expressive, and contains depth
and musical interest." (3) "... the music is
pleasant enough, and with an effective poem, it
might have proved expressive."

B224. Monfried, Walter. "Symphony's Premiere of 'Festive
Ode' Rates Praise." Milwaukee Journal, October 4,
1966.

Review of the premiere of Festive Ode (W65). "Ward
is modern in outlook, but he is not afraid of
tunefulness and he drives to the heights in
exhilarating fashion. He is not only highly
capable and clever in his craft, but he is
thoroughly and unmistakably American."

B225. Montgomery, Diana. "Opera Singer Typifies New Breed."
Seattle Post-Intelligencer, January 29, 1968.

Interview with Mary Leuders, who sings the role of
Elizabeth Proctor in the Seattle Opera production
of The Crucible (W55t).

B226. Morgan, Marta. "Six Operas in S.F. Spring Season."
       San Jose (Calif.) Mercury-News, January 10, 1965.

       Preview of a performance of The Crucible by the San
       Francisco Opera (W55o).

B227. Morrison, Don. "Composer Conducts Own Composition as
       Highlight of Concert by Symphony." Sioux City
       (Iowa) Journal, February 18, 1963.

       Review of a performance of Symphony No. 2 by the
       Sioux City Symphony Orchestra (W31h). "The Ward
       symphony is vibrant and virile and intensely
       romantic. The composer shows a good sense of the
       dramatic."

B228. Murphy, Carol Eve. "An Analysis of the Sacred Songs
       for Pantheists for Soprano with Piano or Orchestral
       Accompaniment, by Robert Ward." Unpublished
       Master's thesis, Eastman School of Music, 1963.

       Lengthy analysis of the Sacred Songs for Pantheists
       (W42), with particular attention to issues of
       interest to performers. "But despite the technical
       problems [of performance], this composer has
       written very singable melodies which flow freely
       between the accompaniment and vocal lines. The
       songs will present a challenge to the more
       experienced singer and show a definite growth in
       Ward's style as a vocal composer."

B229. Nelson, Boris. "Toledo-Bound Opera, Based on
       'Crucible,' Work of a Melodist." Toledo (Ohio)
       Blade, January 17, 1971.

       Preview of a performance of The Crucible by the
       Toledo Opera Association (W55cc), with an interview
       with the composer.

B230. "Opera 'Crucible' Opens at S.U.I." Iowa City (Iowa)
       Press-Citizen, August 1, 1962.

       Review of a performance of The Crucible at the
       State University of Iowa (W55d). "... it is
       virtually impossible to grasp at one hearing the
       full range of emotional ideas compressed in it."

B231. "Orchestra Conducted by Barnett." Rochester (N.Y.)
       Democrat and Chronicle, January 31, 1958.

       Review of a performance of the Third Symphony by
       the Rochester Philharmonic Orchestra (W39e). "It is
       in three well thought out movements, in frankly
       romantic vein and including a particularly
       appealing arioso theme. If nothing particularly
       important seems to happen in the course of the
       music, it is always agreeable and shows the mark of
       high musicianship, a work of individuality and

taste."

B232. O´Reilly, F. Warren. "´The Crucible´ Gets Fine
       Performance." <u>Miami (Fla.) News</u>, March 14, 1974.

       Review of a performance of <u>The Crucible</u> by the
       Greater Miami International Opera (W5511). "Ward´s
       music for this all-too-true page of our history
       relies mostly on solo voices to project the drama
       in lyrically phrased recitatives."

B233. [Pan American Union.] "Robert Ward." <u>Compositores de
       América/Composers of the Americas</u> 9 (1963).

       Brief biography, in English and Spanish, and
       worklist.

B234. Pantell, Hope. "Moiseiwitsch at Lyric." unidentified
       newspaper, February 25, 1948.

       Review of a performance of the <u>First Symphony</u> by
       the National Symphony Orchestra (W16c). "It is in
       many respects an impressive job, more notable for
       expert workmanship, harmonic and instrumental, than
       for strength and originality of musical ideas."

B235. Parmenter, Ross. "´The Crucible´ Is Presented at City
       Center." <u>New York Times</u>, March 26, 1962.

       Review of a performance of <u>The Crucible</u> by the New
       York City Opera (W55b). "Emerson Buckley, the
       conductor, worked hard to see that the music
       underlined the play´s most dramatic moments, and it
       did this most effectively during the visionary
       moments of the trial scene."

B236. Parmenter, Ross. "Music: Ward Symphony." <u>New York
       Times</u>, March 18, 1959.

       Review of a performance of the <u>Fourth Symphony</u> by
       the National Orchestral Association (W52b). "[The]
       work, for all the skillful manipulation of its
       material, had little individuality of statement or
       originality of invention."

B237. Parmenter, Ross. "Music World: Colorado´s ´Lady´ is
       Katie." <u>New York Times</u>, May 3, 1964.

       Preview of the premiere of <u>The Lady from Colorado</u>
       (W60a).

B238. Parmenter, Ross. "Opera: ´The Lady from Colorado´."
       <u>New York Times</u>, July 27, 1964.

       Review of the premiere of <u>The Lady from Colorado</u>
       (W60a). "And the music, far from having the naivete
       of genuine innocence, has the professionalism of
       opera composers turning to a ´Paint Your Wagon´

type Broadway show."

B239. Paysour, LaFleur. "´Abelard and Heloise´ in World
       Premiere at Ovens Auditorium." <u>Charlotte (N.C.)</u>
       <u>Observer</u>, February 21, 1982.

       Review of the premiere of <u>Abelard and Heloise</u>
       (W78a). "[The] score blends rich orchestration and
       melodious vocal writing to good effect. Though
       he´s skimply on the use of big, memorable arias,
       Ward sets up a parade of brief solos and duets that
       cover the musical gamut.... [T]he score spills
       chants, ballads, tightly harmonized choruses and
       complex jazz rhythms."

B240. Paysour, LaFleur. "Saxophone Concerto Premieres."
       <u>Charlotte (N.C.) Observer</u>, February 16, 1984.

       Review of the premiere of the <u>Concerto for</u>
       <u>Saxophone</u> (W81a). "Robert Ward has given it [the
       tenor saxophone] a score that puts it in the
       driver´s seat.... It runs through jazz, the blues,
       big band era swing and lots of neo-romantic strains
       for the strings.... On first hearting, the
       elements didn´t exactly clash; they simply didn´t
       mesh tightly."

B241. Penniman, Helen A.F. "Peabody Concert Features the
       Works of Robert Ward." <u>Baltimore News Post</u>,
       February 14, 1951.

       Review of a performance of <u>Sonata No.1 (W40c)</u>, <u>Folk</u>
       <u>Dance (W19a)</u>, <u>Lamentation (W30d)</u>, <u>Angels (W19a)</u>, <u>As</u>
       <u>I Watched the Ploughman Ploughing</u> (W10d), <u>Vanished</u>
       (W17c), <u>Rain Has Fallen All the Day</u> (W13c), <u>Sorrow</u>
       <u>of Mydath</u> (W9e), <u>Intoxication</u> (W42b), <u>Scherzo</u>
       (W41a), and the <u>Third Symphony</u> (39b) at the Peabody
       Institute. "[The Symphony] is an assured and solid
       score, whose theme is firmly voiced by the
       woodwinds ... To this listener, the Scherzo ...
       stood second in musical worth. No uncertainty
       here, the composer immediately seized and expressed
       his inspiration.... [In the songs,] Mr. Ward´s
       vocal intervals are too wide, he does not write so
       well ,for voice as for piano.... As it appeared to
       us, the violin-piano sonata needs reworking, to
       provide a better balance between the
       instruments..."

B242. Perkins, Francis D. "´He Who Gets Slapped´ Has N.Y.
       City Opera Premiere." <u>New York Herald Tribune</u>,
       April 13, 1959.

       Review of a performance of <u>He Who Gets Slapped</u> by
       the New York City Opera Company (W46b). "The music
       speaks well for Mr. Ward´s operatic
       craftsmanship.... The score, as a rule, is frankly
       melodic, and avoids heavy-treading musical speech.

Besides lyric recitative and arioso, it has a
liberal assortment of arias or their counterpart."

B243.   P[erkins], F[rancis] D.   "Robert Ward Composition
Heard Here." New York Herald Tribune, March 17,
1959.

Review of a performance of the Fourth Symphony by
the National Orchestral Association (W52b). "Its
musical ideas are frankly and appealingly melodic,
and there is a pervasive liveliness in the main
part of the first movement and in the finale ...
[The] themes are rather overworked, and the
orchestra is kept briskly busy all too constantly."

B244.   Pinel, Stephen.   "ASO Premiers Ward, Offers
Prokofieff." Albany (N.Y.) Jewish World [?], May 7,
1980.

Review of a performance of the Fourth Symphony by
the Albany Symphony Orchestra in Albany (W52c,
W52d). "Ward knows how to write for orchestra,
using the strings to blanket the audience with lush
harmony while the winds are intermittently used for
color, in a French way."

B245.   Porter, Andrew.   "Serious Matters." New Yorker 58, no.
18 (June 21, 1982): 104-107.

Review of the premiere of Minutes till Midnight
(W79a). "Ward´s music -- melodious, fluent,
eclectic, made from memories of Puccini, of Richard
Rodgers, of Kurt Weill -- is undistinguished."

B246.   Purcell, Trip.   "Musical Drama to End Summerstage
Season." Durham (N.C.) Morning Herald, July 22,
1981.

Preview of a performance of Claudia Legare in
Durham (W75b).

B247.   Purcell, Trip.   "Production of ´Claudia LeGare´ [sic]
Marks Start of Musical Theater." Durham (N.C.)
Morning Herald, July 24, 1981.

Preview of a performance of Claudia Legare in
Durham (W75b).

B248.   "Rachel Bloom is Guest Soloist of Symphony." Nyack
(N.Y.) Journal-News, March 4, 1958.

Review of a performance of Jonathon and the Gingery
Snare by the Suburban Symphony of Rockland (W38e).
"... a nonsense suite, tickling the risibilities of
the small fry and winning the admiration of all by
its clever use of association, sometimes quite
obvious and sometimes off-beat and, therefore,
extra amusing."

B249. Reno, Doris. "´The Crucible´ Proves a Hard-Hitting
       Opera." <u>Miami Herald</u>, c.August 20, 1966.

       Review of a performance of <u>The Crucible</u> by the Lake
       George Opera Festival (W55p). "The music is
       certainly hard-hitting and full of relentless
       tension..."

B250. RePass, Richard. [untitled review] <u>Opera</u> 13 (1962):
       25-27.

       Review of the premiere of <u>The Crucible</u> (W55a).
       "The strengths of Ward´s score lie in the musical
       characterizations of the many personalities which
       throng the opera, and in his careful building of
       dramatic climaxes."

B251. RePass, Richard. [untitled review] <u>Opera</u> 10 (1959):
       518.

       Review of a performance of <u>He Who Gets Slapped</u> by
       the New York City Opera (W46b). "Its music is
       modern, fresh, subtly scored, tuneful, and
       dramatic."

B252. Rich, Alan. "Another Version of ´Cosi fan tutte,
       Plus Some Operas New to Disks." <u>New York Times</u>,
       April 21, 1963.

       Review of the recording of <u>The Crucible</u> (D5). "Its
       musical material is quite obviously derivative from
       a number of older operatic styles, and does not
       always coalesce into an experience worthy of the
       Arthur Miller play it attempts to underline. But
       there is a great deal of excitement, however
       superficial, in the ensemble writing."

B253. Rich, Alan. "Forging an Opera from Miller´s
       ´Crucible´." <u>New York Times</u>, October 22, 1961.

       Interview with the composer on the occasion of the
       premiere of <u>The Crucible</u> (W55a).

B254. "Robert Ward Succeeds Cramer as Galaxy Managing
       Editor." <u>Musical America</u> 76, no. 8 (June 1956):
       23.

       News story on Ward´s appointment as managing editor
       of Galaxy Music Corporation.

B255. "Robert Ward´s New Opera Premiered in Charlotte."
       <u>Symphony Magazine</u> 33, no. 1 (February/March 1982):
       40-41.

       Interview with the composer on the occasion of the
       premiere of <u>Abelard and Heloise</u> (W78a).

B256. Roos, James. "The Crucible: American (Conservative)
       Opera Makes Miami Appearance." Miami Herald,
       c.March 10, 1974.

       General discussion of contemporary American opera
       on the occasion of a performance of The Crucible by
       the Greater Miami International Opera (W5511).
       "What do you term such operas? Stamp them
       'traditionalist' or 'folk opera' in sound and
       style, and plainly representative of what Americans
       have created and continue to offer the public. And
       count 'The Crucible' among them."

B257. Roos, James. "New World Festival of the Arts: It
       Didn't Help the Tourist Trade, but the Premieres
       Were Exciting." High Fidelity 32, no. 11 (November
       1982): 24-26.

       Review of the premiere of Minutes till Midnight
       (W79a). "The music echoed everything from Puccini
       to Copland, with even a hint of Broadway, and
       Ward's harp-strewn orchestration sounded oddly
       outmoded considering the subject."

B258. Roos, James. "Powerful Performances Carry 'The
       Crucible'." Miami Herald, March 13, 1974.

       Review of a performance of The Crucible by the
       Greater Miami International Opera (W5511). "Ward's
       score is big and brawny, sometimes soaringly
       beautiful, though a sop to conservative ears. It
       has its moments and its points, but its sameness
       throughout deadens impact. In the end, the
       emotional tension felt throughout the evening is
       contingent primarily on the play."

B259. Roos, James. "A Time Whose Play has Come." Miami
       Herald, May 30, 1982.

       Preview of the premiere of Minutes Till Midnight
       (W79a), with an interview with the composer.

B260. S., D. "Two New U.S. Operas." Music Magazine/Musical
       Courier 163, no. 13 (December 1961): 36.

       Review of the premiere of The Crucible (W55a).
       "The extent of the composer's grasp of the operatic
       paraphernalia shows in the deft characterization,
       effective use of ensemble, and careful building of
       climaxes in each scene."

B261. S., H. "Renaissance der Opera in den USA."
       Wiesbadenes Tagblatt (West Germany), October 28,
       1963.

       Preview of a performance of The Crucible by the
       Hessische Staattheater (W55j), with an interview
       with the composer.

B262. S[abin], R[obert]. "Composers Group." _Musical_
       America 77, no. 12 (November 1, 1957): 20.

       Review of a performance of _Sacred Songs for_
       Pantheists by Rosemarie Radman and Emanual Balaban
       (W42d). "Mr. Ward writes knowingly for the voice
       and his richness of harmonic setting is a
       functional element in the songs as a whole."

B263. S[abin], R[obert]. "He Who Gets Slapped." _Musical_
       America 79, no. 6 (May 1959): 8.

       Review of a performance of _He Who Gets Slapped_ by
       the New York City Opera (W46b). "If this work is
       not wholly satisfactory in itself it leaves no
       doubt in the listener's mind that Mr. Ward has a
       fertile vein of lyric invention and that he can
       spin an effective vocal line and accompany it with
       orchestral color and charm."

B264. Sabin, Robert. "New Ford-Commissioned Operas
       Premiered." _Musical America_ 81, no. 12 (December
       1961): 26-27.

       Review of the premiere of _The Crucible_ (W55a). "It
       is stylistically more unified [than _He Who Gets_
       Slapped], and there is clearer adaptation of music
       to the dramatic situation, though this remains a
       problem with this abundant but not always
       discriminating composer."

B265. S[abin], R[obert]. "Third Symphony by Ward Issued."
       Musical America 79, no. 2 (January 15, 1959): 24.

       Review of the _Third Symphony_ (W39). "... there is
       a refreshing honesty and unashamed lyric quality
       about this work. It has bite and rhythmic energy,
       but one does not feel that the composer is
       paralyzed with fear at being thought old-
       fashioned."

B266. Sabin, Robert. "Ward Writes Cello Pieces." _Musical_
       America 80, no. 8 (July 1961): 36.

       Review of _Arioso and Tarantelle_ (W44). "... the
       conciseness of the forms have [sic] helped him to
       write economically and effectively."

B267. Salisbury, Wilma. "Opera's Future Is in Videotape,
       Composer of 'Crucible' Says." _Cleveland Plain_
       Dealer, December 9, 1972.

       Interview with the composer on the occasion of a
       performance of _The Crucible_ at the Cleveland
       Institute of Music (W55hh).

B268. Sargeant, Winthrop. "Big Week." _New Yorker_ 37, no.

38 (November 4, 1961): 179-182.

Review of the premiere of <u>The Crucible</u> (W55a). "His music, though quite accessible to the average listener, is everywhere dignified and nowhere banal. It is continuously expressive, and it intensifies all the nuances of the drama, from anguish and despair to heroic nobility.... This time, he has created an imposing work that will, I suspect, take its place among the classics of the standard repertory."

B269.   Sargeant, Winthrop. "The Crucible." <u>American Record Guide</u> 29 (1963): 509-510, 588.

Review of the recording (D5) and various performances of <u>The Crucible</u>. "... its musical idiom was forthrightly robust, reflecting none of the ´systems´ and technical trickery that have been characteristic of so much bad contemporary music."

B270.   Sargeant, Winthrop. "East and West." <u>New Yorker</u> 35, no. 10 (April 25, 1959): 145-148.

Review of a performance of <u>He Who Gets Slapped</u> by the New York City Opera Company (W46b). "I should unhesitatingly list ´He Who Gets Slapped´ as one of the half-dozen finest operas to emerge from the contemporary ferment among opera composers -- and that is saying a great deal.... Its music displays originality, and speaks with a personal kind of authority, and the composer handles the human voice with affection and shows a remarkable instinct for setting poetic lines to effective melody."

B271.   Sargeant, Winthrop. "Mountain Music." <u>New Yorker</u> 44, no. 4 (March 16, 1968): 161-163.

Review of a performance of <u>The Crucible</u> by the New York City Opera (W55u). "In fact, to me, it is one of the two or three best American operas so far written -- which, to be sure, is not an overwhelming statement.... Its music is masculine, dignified, and capable of rousing emotion, and adds greatly to the stage spectacle instead of being a mere ornament to it."

B272.   Sargeant, Winthrop. "Oops!" <u>New Yorker</u> 35, no. 12 (May 9, 1959): 161-163.

Overview of the New York City Opera Company´s American-opera festival of 1959, including a production of <u>He Who Gets Slapped</u> (W46b). "Robert Ward´s ´He Who Gets Slapped´ was the surprise of the season, and, unless I am very much mistaken, marked the entrance into the operatic arena of a composer who is destined to do great things there."

B273.   Sargeant, Winthrop. "Past, Present, and Future." New
         Yorker 37, no. 7 (April 7, 1962): 172-174.

         Discussion of some contemporary operas, including
         the premiere of The Crucible (W55a). "... the
         beauty, nobility, skill, power, and utter sincerity
         of Mr. Ward's music bowled me over. If a finer
         opera has been written since the days of Strauss
         and Puccini, I have not heard it."

B274.   Sargeant, Winthrop. "The Touch." New Yorker 35, no.
         6 (March 28, 1959): 129-131.

         Review of a performance of the Fourth Symphony by
         the National Orchestral Association (W52b). "Though
         I should not describe Mr. Ward's symphony as a
         great work of art, it was, as today's symphonies
         go, a sturdy, well-constructed, and agreeably
         melodious composition, exhibiting a mastery of
         contrapuntal lines (with an especially fine sense
         of how to keep a bass line moving), a feeling for
         structural climax that depended neither on noise
         nor on superficial tricks of orchestration, and
         invention of a kind that was neither banal nor
         irritating."

B275.   Sayn, Elena de. "Robert Ward's 'Sonata No. 1'
         Receives Perfect Touch from Herbert Sorkin."
         Washington Evening Star, June 12, 1950.

         Review of the premiere of the First Sonata for
         Violin and Piano (W40a). "The composition is a
         rhapsody on a grand scale, imaginative, passionate,
         songful and brilliant."

B276.   Schauensee, Max de. "Brailowsky Is Given Ovation at
         Phila. Orchestra Concert." Philadelphia Evening
         Bulletin, January 28, 1950.

         Review of a performance of Symphony No. 2 by the
         Philadelphia Orchestra (W31d) " ... vigorous and to
         the point. It is solidly scored throughout, and
         can certainly not be charged with musical anemia.
         In fact, it is the antithesis of that skeletal type
         of music, which was considered the only kind one
         could bother with 15 or 20 years ago."

B277.   Schneider, Peter Otto. "Eine effektvolle Oper."
         Musica 18 (1964): 79.

         Review of a performance of The Crucible by the
         Stadttheater Bern (W55k). "Was an Motivierung in
         einselnen und an Aksentuierung des geistigen und
         tendenziösen Hintergrundes abgegeben werden muss,
         wird durch die allein dem musikalischen Theater
         mögliche Steigerund des Emotionellen mehr als
         ausgeglichen."

B278.   Schonberg, Harold C.   "Opera: Robert Ward's 'The
        Crucible'."   New York Times, October 27, 1961.

        Review of the premiere of The Crucible (W55a). "Mr.
        Ward is an experienced composer whose music fails
        to bear the impress of a really inventive mind.
        Melodically his ideas had little distinction, nor
        was there much to convey the hysteria and terror or
        the Salem witch trials around which the play and
        libretto are based."

B279.   Schweitzer, Gottfried.   "Eklektische Oper."   Musica 18
        (1964): 75.

        Review of a performance of The Crucible by the
        Hessisches Stattheater (W55j). "Die verbliebene
        Opernhandlung bot genügend Ansätze für die
        kompositorische Entfaltung des Eklektikers Robert
        Ward. Er beherrscht die Opernpraxis von Wagner bis
        Menotti, seine Musik jedoch schillert unüberhörbar
        in Reminiszenzen und benügt sich vorzugweise mit
        illustrativer Schilderung."

B280.   Shepard, Claudia.   "Oratorio Singers Open a Few Eyes."
        Winston-Salem (N.C.) Sentinel, May 3, 1976.

        Review of a performance of the Fifth Symphony by
        the Charlotte Oratorio Singers in Winston-Salem
        (W73b). "And though the Bicentennial connection of
        the symphony's movements would be tenuous without
        the narration, the considerable flow and power of
        the music suffers under its weight."

B281.   Shepard, Claudia.   "Program Celebrates Composers."
        Winston-Salem (N.C.) Sentinel, April 7, 1976.

        Review of a performance of Sweet Freedom's Song by
        the Winston-Salem Symphony and Chorale (W62f).
        "Ward's music is basic and decidedly 'American'
        without being a fancy copy of antique forms, a
        mistake favored by many other composers."

B282.   Shertzer, Jim.   "Charlotte Opera: Ward 'Abelard and
        Heloise."   High Fidelity 32, no. 5 (June 1982):
        MA20-21.

        Review of the premiere of Abelard and Heloise
        (W78a). "Like Ward's past stage works, the opera
        is an immediately accessible work conceived largely
        in the musical language and theatrical style of the
        late nineteenth and early twentieth centuries."

B283.   Shertzer, Jim.   "Idea for Concert Popular, but
        Performance Is Lacking."   Winston-Salem (N.C.)
        Journal, March 1, 1975.

        Review of a performance of Jonathon and the Gingery
        Snare by the North Carolina School of the Arts

Orchestra (W38g). "The work reminds one of 'Peter and the Wolf,' and if Prokofiev had used percussion instruments for his musical animals, the pieces might be identical."

B284.   Shertzer, Jim. "Orchestra, Chorale Are Good in Festive Works." <u>Winston-Salem (N.C.) Journal</u>, April 7, 1976.

Review of a performance of <u>Sweet Freedom's Song</u> by the Winston-Salem Symphony and Chorale (W62f). "Ward's orchestral and choral setting are happily married to the texts and are by turns stirring, melancholy, defiant and jubilant. The 40-minute piece is somewhat pat, long for its substance and a bit repetitious."

B285.   Shertzer, Jim. "Program Gets Warm Response." Winston-Salem (N.C.) Journal, May 3, 1976.

Review of a performance of the <u>Fifth Symphony</u> by the Charlotte Oratorio Singers in Winston-Salem (W73b). "The sour note ... turned out to be the narration, a sincere but awkward intellectual history of America. ... It is music of the sort that Ward has made his reputation with -- dramatic but conservative."

B286.   Shertzer, Jim. "Ward Leads Arts School Orchestra." <u>Winston-Salem (N.C.) Journal and Sentinel</u>, November 17, 1974.

Review of a performance of <u>Symphony No. 2</u> by the North Carolina School of the Arts Orchestra (W31m). " ... like most works from the post-war period, the symphony has an exuberantly American feel deeply rooted in our greatest native music, jazz and the blues."

B287.   Shertzer, Jim. "Ward's Music Finds Place in Bicentennial." <u>Winston-Salem (N.C.) Journal</u>, March 14, 1976.

Interview with the composer on the occasion of a performance of <u>Sweet Freedom's Song</u> by the Winston-Salem Symphony and Chorale (W62f).

B288.   Shertzer, Jim. "Ward's New Opera: A Tale of Love Skittishly Told." <u>Winston-Salem (N.C.) Journal</u>, February 28, 1982.

Review of the premiere of <u>Abelard and Heloise</u> (W78a). "Ward's music is straightforward, earnest and totally sincere, and his lines show his appreciation for the glory of the human voice. What the opera seems short of is the really big numbers, the arias that typically 'sell' an opera, and the complexities that draw listeners to a second or third hearing."

B289.   Sluder, Rick. "Opera Composer Plays It Low-Key."
        Raleigh (N.C.) News and Observer, April 4, 1982.

        Interview with the composer on the occasion of the
        premiere of Abelard and Heloise (W78a).

B290.   Smith. [untitled review] Variety 307, no. 6 (June 9,
        1982): 72.

        Review of the premiere of Minutes till Midnight
        (W79a). "... some of the most uninspired music to
        be heard by an American composer in recent times."

B291.   Smith, Patrick J. "The Crucible (March 8)." High
        Fidelity 18, no. 6 (June 1968): MA9.

        Review of a performance of The Crucible by the New
        York City Opera (W55u). "Nor is the opera helped
        by Robert Ward's pallid score, precisely the proper
        shade of inoffensive gray that foundations and
        awards committees seize on as significant
        manifestations of American Opera."

B292.   Smith, R.C. "Opera 'The Crucible' Misses Sense of
        Mystery." Durham (N.C.) Morning Herald, January
        12, 1986.

        Review of a performance of The Crucible at Duke
        University (W55zz). "Only great music could
        overcome the dramatic obstacles to provide a
        winning opera here and, while composer Robert
        Ward's music is at times full of charm, it is not
        up to the dramatic eloquence that the story
        demands."

B293.   Smith, Tim. "Minutes-Midnight Was a 'Bomb' in More
        Ways than One." Fort Lauderdale (Fla.) News and
        Sun-Sentinel, June 6, 1982.

        Review of the premiere of Minutes Till Midnight
        (W79a). "What Ward has come up with is little more
        than Broadway show tunes (and terribly dull
        Broadway show tunes at that), separated by warmed
        over 18th century recitative."

B294.   "Snare Drum Piece Hit of Concert." Daytona Beach
        (Fla.) Morning Journal, April 5, 1963.

        Review of a performance of Jonathon and the Gingery
        Snare by the Florida Symphony (W38f). "'Jonathan
        [sic] and the Gingery Snare' by the contemporary
        composer Robert Ward was one of the few numbers for
        which the children actually sat still."

B295.   Southgate, Harvey. "String Group Conquers Contem-
        porary Works." Rochester (N.Y.) Democrat and

Chronicle, November 2, 1966.

Review of a performance of the First String Quartet
by the Cadek Quartet (W63b). "As a student here
Ward showed a gift for lyric simplicity, and some
of this shines through this work, although it has
its atonal and ambiguous moments."

B296.   Spetnagel, Lucy. "This Original Composition Worth
Listening To Again." Kingsport (Tenn.) Times,
February 4, 1979.

Review of a performance of Concerto for Piano and
Orchestra by Marjorie Mitchell and the Kingsport
Symphony Orchestra (W69c). "... the music is
gorgeous with lush harmonies and intriquing [sic]
rhythms reminiscent of Gershwin. Although it is in
traditional form, it reflects ideas which could
only come from this century."

B297.   St., F. "Zurück zur Gesangsoper." Wiesbadenes Kurier
(West Germany), October 26, 1963.

Preview of a performance of The Crucible by the
Hessisches Stattheater (W55j), with an interview
with the composer.

B298.   "Staging the Crucible." Seattle Post-Intelligencer,
January 26, 1968.

Preview of a performance of The Crucible by the
Seattle Opera (W55t), with an interview with the
composer.

B299.   Stambler, Bernard. "Robert Ward." American Composers
Alliance Bulletin 4, no. 4 (1955): 3-11.

Discussion, with some analysis, of Ward's works to
1955, with a catalogue of compositions, a biographical note, and excerpts from reviews. "The
opened-out vistas of his art in the past decade
have only paralleled his development as an individual: his teaching, conducting, administering ...
these are his fulfillments of the function of
man-as-artist.... [A]s a Bach or a Shakespeare
might be puzzled by the inverted snobbery of such a
concept as ´Gebrauchtsmusik,´in much this same way
has Robert Ward demonstrated an idea of craftsmanship, of the efficient and vital performance of a
social and artistic function."

B300.   Steyer, Ralf. [untitled review] Opera 15 (1964): 120.

Review of a performance of The Crucible by the
Hessisches Staattheater (W55j). "... the music
consists of nothing but clichés put together. It
is in every respect without originality (if
occasionally not without pleasantness) and tinkles

along for two-and-a-half hours in the style of
newsreel background music."

B301.   Stockholm, Gail. "Ward´s ´Crucible´ a Real Chiller!"
        Cincinnati Enquirer, January 25, 1971.

        Review of a performance of The Crucible at the
        University of Cincinnati (W55bb). "Ward creates a
        realistic atmosphere of terror running wild in a
        small village as guilt-ridden persons seek
        scapegoats for their own personal and moral
        failures."

B302.   Stowe, George W. "Hartt Opera Dept. Stages ´The
        Crucible´ in English." Hartford (Conn.) Times,
        April 23, 1964.

        Review of a performance of The Crucible at the
        Hartt College of Music (W55l). "For my money it is
        the finest American opera of the century, with a
        libretto good enough to inspire a Verdi or
        Moussorgsky."

B303.   Stromberg, Rolf. "Act Away Opera´s Posy Pretensions."
        Seattle Post-Intelligencer, February 2, 1968.

        Interview with Allen Fletcher, stage director of
        the Seattle Opera production of The Crucible
        (W55t).

B304.   Stromberg, Rolf. "´Crucible´ a Triumph." Seattle
        Post-Intelligencer, February 3, 1968.

        Review of a performance of The Crucible by the
        Seattle Opera (W55t). "But the whole opera has a
        clarity it did not possess before, and Ward´s opera
        gains stature as a contemporary work as a
        result.... And the singers were able to bring out
        the intricate materials in Ward´s lyric score, and
        there are many instances of strained beauty."

B305.   Stromberg, Rolf. "´The Crucible´ Lacks Zest."
        Seattle Post-Intelligencer, February 1, 1968.

        Review of a performance of The Crucible by the
        Seattle Opera (W55t). "Whether it was the chill
        weather outside to blame, the over-all result was
        slow and ponderous, almost without zest or a
        vitality to match these affairs of conscience,
        betrayal and death in Puritan New England."

B306.   Strongin, Theodore. "´The Crucible´ Sung by Hunter
        Players." New York Times, May 5, 1967.

        Review of a performance of The Crucible by the
        Hunter College Opera Workshop (W55r). "Singing,
        acting, staging and designing went right to the
        point, without fuss, without frills. ´The

Crucible,´ based on the Arthur Miller play about the Salem witch trials, flourishes under this kind of treatment. The story carries its own built-in jolt. It doesn´t need trimmings."

B307.   Taggart, Patrick. "Opera as Form Is Favorite for Mr. Ward." Winston-Salem (N.C.) Twin City Sentinel, April 7, 1973.

Interview with the composer on the occasion of a performance of He Who Gets Slapped at the North Carolina School of the Arts (W46d).

B308.   Tajiri, Larry. "Opera Planned on Lady Moon." Denver Post, August 3, 1962.

Preview of the premiere of The Lady from Colorado (W60a); interview with the composer and the librettist.

B309.   Taubman, Howard. "Barzin Closes His Season by Leading the American Orchestra in Three New Works." New York Times, May 21, 1948.

Review of a performance of Jubilation: An Overture (W28) and Adagio and Allegro (W27) by the National Orchestral Association. "[Jubilation is] a work that has a vigorous lift and a personal quality.... It shows that at least one man was not too tired to feel good on Okinawa.... [Adagio and Allegro] is agreeable music, but does not have the snap and exuberance of the overture."

B310.   Taubman, Howard. "Opera: By Robert Ward." New York Times, April 13, 1959.

Review of a performance of He Who Gets Slapped by the New York City Opera Company (W46a). "In some places it conveys an emotion or sets off a dramatic moment strikingly; in others it is commonplace.... Within the framework of a traditional style that calls to mind many influences, Mr. Ward has managed to give the story a personal dimension. When a composer can do that he has not tackled the operatic form in vain."

B311.   Taubman, Howard. "Opera of Promise." New York Times, May 27, 1956.

Review of the premiere of Pantaloon (W46a). "Mr. Ward´s abundance of ideas is disarming. His music pours out with a generosity that is in strong contrast to the barren scores of some other contemporary operas.... He must perfect the art of differentiating his people more sharply through his music. His lyrical bent need not be sacrificed in any way, but it needs to be controlled and disciplined.

B312. Taubman, Howard. "Opera: ´Pantaloon´ Has Its
       Premiere." New York Times, May 18, 1956.

       Review of the premiere of Pantaloon (W46a). "The
       work is dramatic and lyrical; it holds the
       attention and engages one´s sympathies.... But one
       admires the conviction and excitement with which
       this young American writes, and one respects him
       for not straining to be what he is not. His
       musical nature seems to be direct and songful, and
       he has followed his inclinations."

B313. Taylor, Sam. "Top Composer Gets Award, Vyner Leads
       His Last Symphony." Lancaster (Pa.) New Era, April
       30, 1979.

       Review of a performance of the Prairie Overture
       and the second movement of Divertimento for
       Orchestra by the Lancaster Symphony Orchestra
       (W51j, W54e), with an interview with the composer.
       "We liked them! Although they bear the mark of the
       20th century, they are totally shorn of pretension
       of any kind, unfettered by any recogntion [sic] of
       trial balloons of disonance [sic] or avant-garde
       affectation. They rest on a strong, robustly
       romantic, melody line."

B314. Thibodeau, Ralph. "Conductor´s Music Easy to Listen
       to." Corpus Christi (Tex.) Caller-Times, March 6,
       1971.

       Review of a performance of Antiphony for Winds, the
       First String Quartet, the Divertimento for
       Orchestra, and Sweet Freedom´s Song at Del Mar
       College (W68d, W63j, W54d, W62e). "Ward works with
       a modern harmonic and rhythmic vocabulary largely
       within the traditional tonal system, so that his
       music, while vital and contemporary, is easy to
       listen to."

B315. Thomas, Ernst. "Europäische Erstaufführung von Wards
       ´Hexenjagd´." Neue Zeitschrift für Musik 124
       (1963): 487.

       Review of a performance of The Crucible by the
       Hessisches Staattheater (W55j). "Der beste Beweis
       dafur mag sein, dass Ward mit allen Mitteln,
       vokalen und instrumentalen, aufgepulverter Musik,
       nicht die Spannung durchzuhalten vermag, die
       Millers Drama dem Komponisten sozusagen frei Haus
       leifert."

B316. Thomson, Virgil. American Music since 1900. New York:
       Holt, Rinehart and Winston, 1971.

       Biography of Ward, pp. 181-182. Also, of The
       Crucible (W55): "... a solid but not quite first-

class play by Arthur Miller set to solid but not quite first-class music." (p. 63)

B317. Todd, Sharon. "Ward to Conduct Greenville Symphony as Guest Artist." Greenville (S.C.) News, February 19, 1976.

Preview of a performance of Symphony No. 2 by the Greenville Symphony (W31n), with a short interview with the composer.

B318. Toppman, Lawrence. "Opera Premiere Draws Cheers." Charlotte (N.C.) News, February 20, 1982.

News story on the reaction to the premiere of Abelard and Heloise (W78a).

B319. Toppman, Lawrence. "Ovens Acoustics Muffle Premiere of Tuneful Opera." Charlotte (N.C.) News, February 20, 1982. (Also appeared in the Winston-Salem (N.C.) Sentinel on the same day.)

Review of the premiere of Abelard and Heloise (W78a). "Though Mr. Ward claims direct descendence inspirationally from Puccini, he seldom allows a melody line to blossom into an aria. But the entire score, which finds room for elements of plainsong and jazz, falls easily on the ear."

B320. Townsend, Douglas. [untitled review] Notes 10 (1953): 486-487.

Review of the First Sonata for Violin and Piano (W40). "The sonata ... should be included in a well-rounded music library, since, apart from being made available to other prospective performers, it is also a work which is strongly representative of one phase of present-day American music."

B321. Trimble, Lester. "Music." Nation 188 (1959): 463-464.

Review of a performance of He Who Gets Slapped by the New York City Opera Company (W46b). "Without introducing any particulary ironic-sounding musical materials or, indeed, anything more revolutionary than a constant flow of good melody, harmony and rhythm, he conveyed in the first two acts a disturbing sense that life behind the scenes of a small, Parisian circus -- and on the outside as well -- was a sick morass of bitterness, heading inevitably toward an ugly tragedy."

B322. Trump, Peter. "Composer, Chamber Artists Win Generous Applause." Albany (N.Y.) Times-Union, May 6, 1980.

Review of a performance of the First String Quartet and the First Sonata by the Capitol Chamber Artists

(W63k, W401). Of the Quartet: "Always accessible, this music does not seem to bear the stamp of any particular period or influence, but partakes of all to make its own impression. Harmonic textures give way to rhapsodic lyricism, all smoothly integrated in a balanced structure." Of the Sonata: "... there is a thread of jazziness woven through it which keeps things lively. But he doesn't get bogged down and let anything dominate too much."

B323. Trump, Peter. "Julius Hegyi's Figaro Overture Scintillates." Albany (N.Y.) Times-Union, May 5, 1980.

Review of a performance of the Fourth Symphony by the Albany Symphony Orchestra in Albany (W52d). "Ward's music, as he says, does have a basic jazziness which is attractive without distracting from the serious intent."

B324. Tyler, Phyllis. "Robert Ward and Robert Anderson: 'We're Trying to Excite the Imagination of the Public'." Durham (N.C.) Independent, May 7-20, 1987.

Interview with the composer on the occasion of the premiere of Dialogue on the Tides of Time (W86a).

B325. "U.S. Opera Composers Produce and Talk." Music Magazine/ Musical Courier 163, no. 11 (October 1961): 7-8, 48.

Interview with Peggy Glanville-Hicks, Vittorio Giannini, Douglas Moore, and Robert Ward. Ward's section deals largely with The Crucible (W55).

B326. Valicenti, Joe. "Doomwatch." Opera 33 (1982): 1167-1168.

Review of the premiere of Minutes till Midnight (W79a). "Ward's music disappoints in that it treats such cataclysmic subjects ... with an almost operetta-like lyricism and floridness."

B327. Valicenti, Joe. "'Minutes' Offers Much to Admire in World of Opera." Miami News, June 5, 1982.

Review of the premiere of Minutes Till Midnight (W79a). "One senses that the music is too lyrical and sweet to underscore such mind-boggling consequences as global destruction and the annihilation of mankind."

B328. "Violin and Piano." Musical Courier 145, no. 8 (April 15, 1952): 30.

Review of the First Sonata for Violin and Piano (W40). "There is skillful interweaving in the duet

of instruments and a graciousness of character in
the many richly cantabile passages."

B329. Wadsworth, Stephen. [untitled review] Opera News 42,
no. 20 (April 8, 1978): 62.

Review of a performance of He Who Gets Slapped by
the Encompass Theatre (W46e). "Ward's music is
always nimble, often lovely, occasionally moving,
seldom striking."

B330. Wallace, Dean. "Memorable Music Theater." San
Francisco Chronicle(?), June 22, 1965.

Preview of a performance of The Crucible by the San
Francisco Opera (W55o). "... Ward manages to do
three difficult jobs equally well: delineation of
character, evocation of mood, and creation of
dramatic opinion."

B331. Wallace, Weldon. "Heifetz at Lyric." Baltimore Sun,
February 15, 1951.

Review of a performance including Adagio and
Allegro by the Baltimore Symphony (see W27e). "The
novelty of the occasion, 'Adagio and Allegro,' by
Robert Ward, is a romantic work, existing in an
almost pure Sibelius atmosphere -- and better than
some Sibelius. ... Though not particularly
individual, it is excellent in construction and
rich in feeling."

B332. Wallace, Weldon. "National Symphony." Baltimore Sun,
February 25, 1948.

Review of a performance of the First Symphony by
the National Symphony Orchestra (W16c). "Mr. Ward's
symphony ... seems an able and interesting work.
Its harmonic color and general atmosphere suggest
Sibelius. The composer has treated his themes
along lines developed in the late Nineteenth
Century."

B333. Walsh, Michael. "Professional Touch in 'Crucible'."
Rochester (N.Y.) Democrat and Chronicle, December
14, 1973.

Review of a performance of The Crucible by the
Eastman Opera Theatre (W55kk). "Simply because an
operatic production features student singers and a
student orchestra does not necessarily mean it will
not achieve an artistic result that is
indistinguishable from professionalism. I offer
last night's presentation ... as proof."

B334. Ward, Robert. See also B355 (Where Is Our American
Music?) and B358 (Williams, David Russell).

B335. Ward, Robert E. "Action for Art." College Music
       Symposium 16 (1976): 9-11.

       The composer's remarks on the need for solidarity
       among musicians in a time when tax money is being
       increasingly withdrawn from the arts.

B336. Ward, Robert. "The American Composers Alliance: Who?
       What? How?" American Composers Alliance Bulletin
       11, no. 2-4 (December 1963): 4.

       Discussion of the work of the American Composers
       Alliance.

B337. Ward, Robert. "Composers in Uniform." Modern Music
       23 (1946): 108-110.

       Report on the work of various composers for the
       U.S. armed forces in World War II.

B338. Ward, Robert. "Letter from the Army." Modern Music
       20 (1943): 170-174.

       The composer's account of his experiences with, and
       reactions to, music in the U.S. Army, with
       particular attention to The Life of Riley (W23).

B339. Ward, Robert. "More Seasonal Notes." Modern Music 18
       (1941): 173-175.

       Review of a number of recent performances of modern
       music.

B340. Ward, Robert. "The Present Situation in the Musical
       Performing Arts." National Association of Teachers
       of Singing Bulletin 20, no. 4 (May 1964): 2-4.

       The composer's comments on the need for a system of
       regional musical production units like those in
       Germany.

B341. Ward, Robert. "Quick-Sketch of Spain." Modern Music
       19 (1942): 142-143.

       Review of Gilbert Chase, The Music of Spain (New
       York: Norton, 1941).

B342. Ward, Robert. "A Story of Symbiotic Genius: The Birth
       of Robert Ward's 'The Crucible'." Listen (Program
       Guide to WUNC radio, Chapel Hill, N.C.), January
       1986: 5-9.

       The composer's account of the writing of The
       Crucible (W55) and its subsequent history.

B343. Ward, Robert. "Training the Composer and Writer for
       the Music Theater." In Perspectives: Creating and
       Producing Contemporary Opera and Musical Theater

(Washington: Opera America, 1983), 27-30.

Discussion by the composer of the necessity for
training young composers in the rudiments of
writing for the theater.

B344.   Ward, Robert. "You´re in the Army Now." Modern Music
        19 (1942): 167-168.

        The composer´s account of his experiences at Fort
        Riley, Kansas.

B345.   Ward, Robert, and Bernard Stambler. "Writing an Opera
        is Collaborative Effort." New York Times, May 13,
        1956.

        Article about their collaboration on the score to
        Pantaloon (W46).

B346.   "Ward, Robert (Eugene)." Current Biography Yearbook,
        1963: 456-458.

        Detailed biography of the composer through the
        early 1960s.

B347.   "Ward, Robert. Fantasia for Brass Choir and Tympani."
        Brass Quarterly 1 (1957): 117-118.

        Review of Fantasia for Brass Choir and Timpani (W).
        "His writing is always richly sonorous, and his
        choice of instruments impeccable. But no amount of
        brilliant scoring can salvage much from the aimless
        procession of themes and motives, the insipid
        harmonies, the frustrated cadences and abortive
        climaxes which make this fantasia more like a bad
        dream."

B348.   "Ward´s ´Crucible´ Comes Home to New England."
        American Composers Alliance Bulletin 11, no. 1
        (June 1963): 12.

        Summary of critical reation to a performance of The
        Crucible at the New England Conservatory (W55f).

B349.   "Ward´s Opera to Make Korean Debut." Durham (N.C.)
        Sun, July 13, 1985.

        News story on a performance of The Crucible in
        Seoul (W55yy), with a short interview with the
        composer.

B350.   Warnke, Frank J. [untitled review] Opera News 32,
        no. 20 (March 16, 1968): 28.

        Review of a performance of The Crucible by the
        Seattle Opera (W55t). "The first two acts ... are
        composed in a fundamentally conservative yet
        flexible and expressive idiom; however, the

composer's curious reluctance to write for more
than one voice at a time slows down the action,
making the work a play with background music."

B351. Watt, Douglas. "'Crucible' Flames as an Opera." New
York Daily News, October 27, 1961.

Review of the premiere of The Crucible (W55a). "His
new score is both melodious and passionate and
rises to the script's most dramatic moments with
exciting thrust. It may not be quite a masterpiece
but it is very close to being one."

B352. Weigle, Carol. "Composer Thinks Children Should Be
Exposed to Music." Erie (Pa.) Daily Times,
November 17, 1958.

Interview with the composer on the occasion of a
performance of the First Symphony by the Erie
Philharmonic Orchestra (W16d).

B353. Weld, Larry. "Music Festival Opens at Eastman."
Rochester (N.Y.) Times-Union, April 30, 1947.

Review of a performance of Hush'd Be the Camps
Today at the Eastman School of Music (see W12c).
"It conveys a deep feeling of sorrow and loss
effectively but never bogs down in an excessive,
maudlin despair."

B354. Werlé, Frederick. [untitled review] Musical Courier
159, no. 6 (May 1959): 11.

Review of the Third Symphony (W39). "It is
admirable for its honesty and sincerity, and
contains many beautiful solo passages, especially
in the slow movement."

B355. Where Is Our American Music? Charleston, S.C.: Piccolo
Spoleto, 1983.

Summary of panel discussion featuring Ward among
various other authorities on American music.

B356. White, Peregrine. "Robert Ward's 'Crucible' Is
'Bewitching'." Durham (N.C.) Sun, January 10,
1986.

Review of a performance of The Crucible at Duke
University (W55zz). "... an unending stream of
extremely subtle chords, phrases -- fascinating
flights of orchestration."

B357. Wiggers, Alvin S. "English Pianist Brings Verve to
Symphony Concert." Nashville Tennessean, January
26, 1949.

Review of a performance of Symphony No. 2 by the

Nashville Symphony Orchestra (W31c). "In the second movement there are traces of melody, but in the first movement, where one terrific blast is played 12 times, and in the third part, which reminded one of ´Custer´s Last Stand,´ the din was terrific."

B358. Williams, David Russell. "Howard Hanson (1896-1981)." Perspectives of New Music 20 (1981): 12-25.

Eulogy to Hanson, including tributes from some former students. Ward´s contribution is on p. 25.

B359. Willis, Thomas. [untitled review] High Fidelity 35, no. 9 (September 1985): MA18-19.

Review of a performance of The Crucible by the Chicago Opera Theater (W55xx). "... Ward´s score communicates at least as well as its source drama, with soaring vocal lines, lush orchestral underpinning, and an expert´s command of English declamation."

B360. Wise, Jim. "Abelard & Heloise: Opera at Duke." Durham (N.C.) Morning Herald, February 19, 1982.

Interview with the composer on the occasion of the premiere of Abelard and Heloise (W78a).

B361. Wise, Jim. "Opera Returns to Durham: The Crucible." Durham (N.C.) Morning Herald, January 3, 1986.

Interview with the composer on the occasion of a performance of The Crucible at Duke University (W55zz).

B362. Wise, Jim. "12th-Century Drama Subordinates Opera´s Music." Durham (N.C.) Morning Herald, February 26, 1982.

Review of the premiere of Abelard and Heloise (W78a). "Ward´s music provides commentary on the action, heightening drama, making ironic counterpoint or foreshadowing the tragedies to come.... The music remains subordinate to the drama..."

B363. "´Witchcraft´ Featured in Opera." Muncie (Ind.) Ball State News, June 23, 1963.

Preview of a performance of The Crucible by the Little Shoestring Opera Workshop (W55h).

B364. Woliver, Charles Patrick. "Robert Ward´s The Crucible: A Critical Commentary." Unpublished D.M.A. thesis, University of Cincinnati, 1986.

Long analysis and discussion of The Crucible (W55),

with biographical and historical notes. "... a
well-constructed operaic materpiece both musically
and dramatically. It deserves, along with certain
works by Menotti, Floyd, Argento, Pasatieri, and
Musgrave, to be placed in a list with the greatest
operas America has to offer."

B365.   Wolter, Beverly. "Opera by Duke's Ward Stars in Miami
        Festival." Durham (N.C.) Morning Herald, June 11,
        1982.

        Interview with the composer on the occasion of the
        premiere of Minutes till Midnight (W79a).

B366.   Wolter, Beverly. "Pulitzer Winning Composer Now
        Teaches Music at Duke." Durham (N.C.) Morning
        Herald, October 28, 1979.

        News story, with an interview, on Ward's joining
        the faculty at Duke University.

B367.   Wolter, Beverly. "Ward's New Opera Deals with Nuclear
        Dilemma." Durham (N.C.) Morning Herald, June 6,
        1982.

        Interview with the composer about his operas, on
        the occasion of the premiere of Minutes Till
        Midnight (see W79a).

B368.   Wolter, Beverly. "Words Are Familiar; Tunes Are Not."
        Winston-Salem (N.C.) Journal, May 20, 1968.

        Interview with the composer on the occasion of a
        performance of Sweet Freedom's Song by the Singers'
        Guild (W62d).

B369.   "World Premiere for Ward Opera." New York Times, July
        5, 1964.

        Review of the premiere of The Lady from Colorado
        (W60a). "The glittering first-night audience ...
        cheered and applauded throughout the performance,
        and at the final curtain showered the singers with
        Colorado carnations, according to Central City
        custom."

B370.   Young, Allen. "Mr. Ward's Lady." Musical America 84,
        no. 7 (September 1964): 20-21.

        Review of the premiere of The Lady from Colorado
        (W60a). "The melodies are expansive and good-
        natured, its rhythms supple and varied achieving a
        consistently mobile and buoyant texture."

B371.   Young, Allen. "Rocky Mountain Ladies." Opera News
        29, no. 2 (October 17, 1964): 21.

        Review of the premiere of The Lady from Colorado

(W60a). "Ward´s tuneful score, which contains several singable parts, has rhythmic variety and a sense of mobility, though there is little to bank on in its simple harmonic structure."

B372. Zacheis, Les. "SUI Does Well with ´Crucible´." <u>Cedar Rapids (Iowa) Gazette</u>, August 1, 1962.

Review of a performance of <u>The Crucible</u> at the State University of Iowa (W55d). "... at times unwieldy and weighed down with its preponderance of characters. And yet, once it gets off the ground, it delivers some sledgehammer blows of highest dramatic impact."

B373. [untitled review] <u>Time</u> 67, no. 22 (June 28, 1956): 51.

Review of the premiere of <u>Pantaloon</u> (W46a). "Composer Ward´s music resembles Mascagni´s, with thick textures, sweepeing strings and sweet harmonies, and thus <u>Pantaloon</u> has the makings of a successful theater piece. Unfortunately, the drama does not need, or benefit from, the addition of music."

INDEX OF INTERVIEWS

Appendix 1:
List of Works by Genre

OPERAS

He Who Gets Slapped, W46
The Crucible, W55
The Lady from Colorado, W60
Claudia Legare, W75
Abelard and Heloise, W78
Minutes till Midnight, W79

ORCHESTRAL MUSIC

Slow Music for Orchestra, W6
Ode, W7
A Yankee Overture, W11
Andante and Scherzo, W14
First Symphony, W16
Adagio and Allegro, W27
Jubilation -- An Overture, W28
Aria, W29
Symphony No. 2, W31
Concert Music, W33
Serenade for Strings, W34
Night Music, W37
Jonathon and the Gingery Snare, W38
Third Symphony, W39
Euphony for Orchestra, W43
Prairie Overture, W51
Fourth Symphony, W52
Divertimento for Orchestra, W54
Hymn and Celebration, W56
Music for a Celebration, W58
Processional March, W59
Hymn to the Night, W64
Festive Ode, W65
Invocation and Toccata, W67
Concerto for Piano and Orchestra, W69
Concertino for Strings, W71
Sonic Structure, W77
Dialogues for Violin, Cello and Orchestra, W80
Concerto for Saxophone and Orchestra, W81

MISCELLANEOUS

Appendix 2:
Alphabetical Index of Titles

Includes all titles, past and present, of whole pieces, as
well as those of individual movements that have text and
might stand alone. Items in {braces} are not official
titles.

Untitled, W25
Vanished, W17
What thing is this, W3
When Christ Rode into Jerusalem, W48
With Rue My Heart Is Laden, W35
Yankee Overture, A, W11

Index

Page numbers, e.g. p.4, refer to pages in the "Biography," numbers preceded by a "W" to the "Works and Performances" section, numbers preceded by a "D" to the "Discography," and numbers preceded by a "B" to the "Bibliography." Colleges, universities, and other institutions of similar scope are alphabetized by their cities.

ABOUT THE AUTHOR

KENNETH KREITNER is currently completing a Ph.D. program in musico-
logy at Duke University with a dissertation on music in fifteenth-century
Barcelona.

Recent Titles in
Bio-Bibliographies in Music
Series Advisers: Donald L. Hixon and Adrienne Fried Block

Thea Musgrave: A Bio-Bibliography
Donald L. Hixon

Aaron Copland: A Bio-Bibliography
JoAnn Skowronski

Samuel Barber: A Bio-Bibliography
Don A. Hennessee

Virgil Thomson: A Bio-Bibliography
Michael Meckna

Esther Williamson Ballou: A Bio-Bibliography
James R. Heintze

Gunther Schuller: A Bio-Bibliography
Norbert Carnovale

Max Reger: A Bio-Bibliography
William E. Grim

Heitor Villa-Lobos: A Bio-Bibliography
David P. Appleby

Jean Langlais: A Bio-Bibliography
Kathleen Thomerson

Lowell Mason: A Bio-Bibliography
Carol A. Pemberton

Daniel Pinkham: A Bio-Bibliography
Kee DeBoer and John B. Ahouse

Arthur Bliss: A Bio-Bibliography
Stewart R. Craggs

Charles Ives: A Bio-Bibliography
Geoffrey Block

Cécile Chaminade: A Bio-Bibliography
Marcia J. Citron

Vincent Persichetti: A Bio-Bibliography
Donald L. Patterson and Janet L. Patterson